PINK MASTERMIND

YOUR PINKPRINT FOR SUCCESS

Compiled by:
Kim N. Carswell and Felicia Phillips

ASTA
PUBLICATIONS

www.astapublications.com

Copyright © 2015 by Kim N. Carswell and Felicia Phillips

Ordering Information

Quantity Sales. Special discounts are available on bulk purchases by corporations, associations, and others. For details, contact the "Special Sales Department" at the Asta Publications address above.

Individual Sales. Asta Publications books are available through most bookstores. They can be ordered directly from Asta Publications: Tel: 800- 482-4190 www.astapublications.com.

First Printing, Asta Publications, LLC, trade paperback first edition January 2015

Manufactured in the United States of America

ISBN: 13: 978-1-934947-66-1

1. Self Help   2. Career   3. Business   4. Masterminding   5. Women   6. Women in Business   I. Title

Cover and Interior Design by: Persona Affairs, LLC
Compiled by: Kim N. Carswell and Felicia Phillips

DEDICATION

This book is dedicated to the women who are ready to Master Their Minds...

Table of Contents

Introduction
vii

The Pink MasterMind
Felicia Phillips
1

Reframing Failure with Success
Dr. Toni G. Alvarado
15

Success Sharpens Success
Robin White
33

Finding the Way Back to Myself
Tia Buckham-White
49

The Authentic Woman: Silettos, Suits and Sweats™
T. Renee' Smith
65

Investing In Your Brand Value
Kim N. Carswell
81

Conclusion
97

Introduction

Being an exceptional, respected woman in today's world is a difficult goal. It is an arduous task to enable yourself while fulfilling the roles of sister, friend, mother, wife or significant other. This requires time and patience, which are both vanishing commodities. However, through platforms such as mastermind groups, women are able to connect with like-minded peers who understand their positions and the barriers they face on a daily basis. These platforms nurture your need to become a 21st-century woman and help lead you to the level of success you desire. In many cases, this support may only be obtained through connecting with other women who can provide quality expertise and insight to the challenges women face today.

How many times have you longed to find success? How many times have you failed or just given up? Whether you're a woman in the workplace, the CEO of your own business, or occupying the executive suite, you've had that fleeting feeling of longing for success at one time or another and it just doesn't feel good. Gone are the days of looking at what you do. Instead people are looking at who you are in the physical and digital world... What message are you sending to people when you communicate or when you just walk into a room? Being insensitive or aloof is no longer tolerated. People are more in tune with their feelings and want to be effective human beings in society. How do you fit in? What are you doing to bring effective change to your organization or business?

The Truth

Some women do exceptionally well, even if they've lacked having a mentor or partner. But usually the women who have no support get stuck whenever they face a setback or obstacle. One day they may even find themselves saying out loud, "I can't do this anymore by myself!" The power of being exposed to a career sponsor or a coach will enhance the levels of the success you experience. How many times have you said, "I got this; I can do this on my own"? The truth is that you do need help. Having an advisor can reduce your learning curve and allow you to obtain lasting success more effectively.

Being Genuine

It is so refreshing to meet someone who is comfortable with being herself. So many times women feel that they have to be someone different than who they are, when the reality is they're better off just being true to who they are. Being authentic is defined as not being false or copied; it is being genuine or real. To be this woman is to be truly confident in one's own skin, operating holistically and harmoniously. Attaining this may not be an easy task, but it is achievable when you decide to let go of the labels and expectations society places on women. The goal is to define your personal brand according to your terms and aspirations.

Collaborative Thinking

Whoever invented the term "collaborative thinking" was definitely a *thought leader*. This is where people with similar goals harness their expertise and mental resources to address a problem or issue. What a wonderful way to bring together great minds. A mastermind group uses collaborative thinking techniques to access "bigger thinking" or, as Napoleon Hill, author of *Think and Grow Rich* calls it, the "Third Mind." A mastermind group is a combination of like-minded individuals with positive energy and a determination to succeed and who offer their expertise and resources to help each member reach his or her individual objectives. Great leaders like media powerhouse Oprah Winfrey and Facebook's COO Sheryl Sandberg have used proven collaborative thinking tools and techniques to impact the lives of many women. If you are open to sharing ideas and gaining different perspectives to take your business or career to the next level, then we highly suggest joining a mastermind group.

It is our sincere hope that by reading *Pink MasterMind: Your PinkPrint for Success* you will discover a personal road map for working in your purpose. Use the expertise of each of the PinkPrint authors to carve out your own journey for reaching your fullest potential as a professional and/or businesswoman. The pages of this book are filled with hidden treasures you can use to find a new world designed by you.

Felicia Phillips and Kim N. Carswell

The Pink MasterMind
Felicia Phillips

"What the mind of man can conceive and believe, it can achieve."
~Napoleon Hill

Alright already! Why is my friend so adamant about me connecting with this woman? I pick up the phone to call Ms. Kim Carswell and we immediately burst into laughter. Yes, it's obvious she has threatened both of us, but for good reason. We realized in that moment that this was no ordinary connection. Our mutual friend knew something we didn't, but we were about to find out. We talked for over an hour and agreed to meet for lunch. OMG! This woman was a powerful force and she said my magic word, "mastermind!"

I fell in love with "Positive Mental Attitude" books when I left home at 17 to attend college. No one in my household had ever talked about this type of literature and I was fascinated by all of it. I knew after my first encounter that this was how I wanted to live my life. I stumbled across a book called *"Success Through a Positive Mental Attitude"* written by Napoleon Hill and W. Clement Stone. In the book, they described positive mental attitude as *"The right mental attitude comprised of the plus characteristics, symbolized by such words as faith, integrity, hope, optimism, courage, initiative, generosity, tolerance, tact, kindliness, and good common sense."* I thought to myself why weren't my friends and family talking about this? Was I weird for embracing this way of thinking? I couldn't turn back; I was hooked and looking through new lenses at how I would accomplish my dreams. It was all about my attitude.

In those years, Napoleon Hill's *"Think and Grow Rich"* made me feel like I could conquer the world by implementing his philosophy to achieve my true destiny. This was euphoric! I couldn't get enough.

Napoleon Hill described mastermind this way, *"A Mastermind is a unique concept that leverages the collective power of the group, creating a Third Mind."* I began to discover authors and motivational speakers like Les Brown, Zig Ziglar, and Dale Carnegie. They spoke to something deep down in my soul. Growing up in my parent's household, the only person they referenced as a motivational force was Jesus Christ. After reading all of these motivational and masterminding books, I thought to myself that my parents were right to see Jesus Christ as a motivational force, as His 12 disciples were indeed a mastermind group. They came together, brainstormed and developed a strategic plan to spread the Gospel that still lives today. Powerful! However, most people became familiar with the term "Mastermind" from Napoleon Hill's *Think and Grow Rich*. One of my much-loved mastermind quotes comes from an interview Napoleon Hill did with Andrew Carnegie. When Napoleon Hill inquired about Mr. Carnegie's success, he answered with the following: *"It is not my mind, and it is not the mind of any other man on my staff, but the sum total of all these minds that I have gathered around me that constitute a master mind in the steel business."*

Then there was Henry Ford and his friends. Whew! Friends like Alexis Carrel, Charles Lindbergh, Harvey Firestone, and Thomas Edison. Now that's a mastermind group on steroids. Look what emerged from their collective efforts: Ford Motor Company, Firestone, The Father of Electricity, a Nobel prizewinning surgeon and an accomplished aviator. Did you notice all the early references to masterminding were attributed to men? Now with the knowledge and vision I embraced, the universe was possibly giving me the opportunity to participate in masterminding from a different perspective.

You see, I knew at the tender age of nine that I wanted to control my destiny. My examples were my father and uncles, who were all entrepreneurs. They seemed to have a mastermind group of their own. At least, they did all the things mastermind groups are known for, even if they didn't realize it at the time. Each one of them was successful in my eyes. They had brick and mortar stores, people patronizing, while smiling, laughing, and spending money in their businesses. They owned homes, cars, and their kids went to private schools. Most of all, they were happy. Yes, this was the life and I wanted it too! Little did I know what it would take to capture that type of success.

Everything I read and seen up to this point on masterminding and business was from a male perspective. They were privileged, some were educated and well connected; and yes, they were mostly white males. Although these examples of mastermind groups and business owners were very different from me, I was not discouraged. I understood that women still faced challenges with being accepted as leaders, business owners, politicians, and CEOs. Even with organizations advocating for the rights of women, we were still struggling with being paid the same as our male counterparts. According to the Bureau of Labors'

Highlights of Women's Earnings in 2012, *"Among both women and men, median weekly earnings for those working full time in management, business, and financial operations jobs were higher than in any other major occupational category in 2012 ($993 for women and $1,387 for men). Of women in management, business, and financial operations occupations, those who were chief executives, computer and information systems managers, and management analysts had the highest median weekly earnings ($1,730, $1,527, and $1,325, respectively). Among men in this job group, chief executives and architectural and engineering managers had the highest earnings ($2,275 and $2,116, respectively). The second highest paying occupational group for women and men was professional and related occupations ($928 for women and $1,267 for men). Among women in professional and related occupations, those who were pharmacists ($1,871) and lawyers ($1,636) had the highest earnings. For men in professional and related occupations, those who were physicians and surgeons ($2,099), lawyers ($2,055), and pharmacists ($1,879) earned the most"*. These were compelling statistics that could not be overlooked.

Women have been oppressed for centuries, which affects the we are treated by society. It affects our self-esteem and how we make decisions regarding our career, social, and family life. As a country, we try to overcome the stigma by putting programs in place that help women initiatives such as: women certifications for contracts and other diversity programs to address these inadequacies. This is wonderful, but if the people who run these programs don't understand or care about the philosophy, then how much progress can we truly make if we are not aligned in our thinking? Did you know that less than 5% of top corporations have women CEOs? Forbes' World's Billionaires 2014 list reported that slightly more than 10% of the 1,645 billionaires that made the list were women. This further justifies the need for women to begin to participate in collaborative think tanks in order to empower themselves socially and economically.

With all of these facts and statistics stating the obvious need for change, I felt in my gut that professional women brainstorming together could be the difference. This vision needed help. It was time for the champion within each of us to step forward in order for change to occur.

Being A Visionary Leader with A Vision

Creative, idealistic, insightful, enterprising, and dreamers are all words used to describe being a leader and a visionary.

During a premarital counseling session, my Pastor described me as resourceful person. Even though, I had my own meaning of the word, I could hardly wait to get home to look up the definition online. The word resourceful is defined as "Having the ability to find quick and clever ways to overcome difficulties." This definition defines what it means to be a visionary.

Wow, I had to laugh. That is exactly how my friends and family had fondly described me over the years. I guess I've been a visionary since the day I was born. My Mom would say, "This girl's got big dreams!" and she was right. Visionaries are clear, concise and lead with integrity. They have the ability to connect with others at a deeper level because they first have a connection with their own inner spirit. They possess an energy that is intoxicating when in its presence. Visionaries have a need to fulfill their passion for something better. However, when you have a vision, the one thing you must realize is that it takes the help of others for it to become visible. You're not the operational person; you're the change agent, thought leader and history maker. It is important that you have the help of those who believe and understand your vision in order for it to manifest properly.

I love reading about female visionaries who embrace positive change. One true Visionary is Kimberly Bryant, Executive Director of Black Girls Code. Kimberly was featured as one of CNN's Visionary Women for her commitment in bridging the technology gap by teaching girls of color computer programming and entrepreneurial skills. Her goal is to reach 1 million girls by 2040. What an audacious goal! Bryant said in her interview with CNN, "I'm doing something to make the world a better place." Visionaries don't operate with a spirit of fear. They operate with confidence. They understand that in order to fulfill their vision they must take risks and go against the mainstream to create positive outcomes. They are considered selfless and driven. They understand that it is more advantageous to be ahead of the curve instead of behind it. That's vision. Look at Fashion Icon and Visionary, Coco Chanel. Chanel took her vision and revolutionized the fashion world for women. She introduced a fashion-forward mindset that still remains relevant today. Regardless of the obstacles women faced during the early 1900s, she pressed on to become a part of fashion history.

Visionaries just don't quit, giving up is not an option. You have to first believe in yourself and your ability to succeed. Your self-confidence is vital; it cannot waiver through the process. If you don't see yourself in action when you close your eyes, then you don't believe it. You must see it in your mind's eye.

There are a few key factors that are important to your success as a Visionary. Have a plan that defines what your vision is to keep you on track. Sometimes you can get carried away with ideas; this will help you stay focused. Next, a Visionary understands that it is advantageous to create their own personal board of advisors when implementing their vision. These are people that can be trusted with your vision and will hold you accountable in achieving your goal and purpose. They are a group that can open doors and provide opportunities that will allow you to manifest your idea.

Then there is your own energy and passion. It is imperative to speak with passion and enthusiasm when you begin to share your vision. People become captivated when you are authentic and purposeful in your delivery. Pink Power is a meeting place for women leaders to participate in a day of mastermind sessions where they can share their individual resources and ideas to help empower one another. When I share the mission of Pink Power, people quickly realize that this vision is a movement. You must be passionate in your pursuit, but tempered with patience. Rome wasn't built in a day... Just remember to stay focused on building momentum and sticking to your plan. Don't forget your vision is your legacy. Your legacy lives on and has the ability to empower others to achieve and believe in what you have created, even when you are no longer the messenger.

Pink Power: A MasterMind Conference for Women

I was excited to meet Kim because I felt comfortable sharing my vision with her. Not everyone will be worthy of your vision in its early stages, but with Kim, I knew in my heart she would be ready to receive it.

The day had come for us to finally meet and brainstorm on the significance of us working together. After our initial conversation, I felt the significance of us coming together would be to provide a platform that would be life changing for women globally. You could see the excitement in our eyes. We were like little girls on a play date with much to discover. We knew something "great" was about to unfold, but little did we both know what that something "great" was going to be. Like most people when meeting for the first time, we talked about our accomplishments in business and life, our goals for the future, and what our legacy would be as mothers and women in business. Then we looked at each other and I said to Kim, "Why are we here?" What was so important that our friend thought we needed to connect? We paused and I felt as if I was being pushed to say something. I began to share with Kim a dream I had of bringing women together to mastermind on a large platform: a conference. She smiled…she smiled really big. Not only were we on the same page, we were on the same paragraph. She talked about her relationships with organizations and her expertise with branding.

After sharing our talents and dreams for women, our new mission was revealed. That was the magic, the reason the universe and our mutual friend had brought us together. In that instance we confirmed it. Kim and I agreed to develop a platform that would close the gap between women in business and women in the workplace, a mastermind conference for women. Yes…Yes…Yes! I left thinking, "Is this really going to happen? If it is, I'm glad I have a partner that truly understands the importance of this much needed platform."

We were fulfilling a passion that was deep inside us, but we were very aware this would be no small undertaking. Now it was time to lay not just the blueprint but the pinkprint!

The name was simple, powerful, and clear, Pink Power: A MasterMind Conference for Women.

We strategized on the "when," "where," and "how" and the importance of our mission and message. It is one thing to visualize, another to implement. We began to reach out to other people and organizations with like-minded missions who would be willing to align themselves with our platform.

After weeks of deliberating on this decision, we began to design the layout, the PinkPrint for our mastermind conference. Our goal was to provide women of different industries and backgrounds the opportunity to have open dialogue about the challenges they faced as women, how to overcome them and create economic opportunity and growth within their individual organizations. This was definitely a game changer.

We understood that the campaign for the advancement of women has increased over time, but there is still much work left to do. According to the National Association of Women Business Owners (NAWBO), women are employing nearly 7.9 million people, and generating $1.4 trillion in sales as of 2014. They also own more than 9.1 million firms. NAWBO went on to report that women-owned firms (50% or more) account for 30% of all privately held firms and contribute 14% of employment and 11% of revenues. Lastly, over the past seven years, the overall increase of 8.3 million (net) new jobs is comprised of a 9.2 million increase in employment in large publicly traded corporations, combined with a

893,000 decline in employment among smaller privately held companies. This means there is more opportunity for women to make their mark on our economy.

Chief Operating Officer of Facebook, Sheryl Sandberg, authored "Lean In: Women, Work and the Will to Lead," a powerful read on where we are as women in the workplace and in society. Business Insider highlighted some of the statistics from Sandberg's book. Statistics show that women hold 16% of board seats and only 18% of women serve in Congress. It also went on to say that in 1970, women were paid $0.59 for every dollar men made. Today, it's $0.77. But the one that struck home with me was this: in a survey of 4000 employees at big companies, 36% of men said they wanted to be CEO and only 18% of women said the same. BAM! It's a mindset. We have to change our way of thinking. The mind is the master. Everything starts with an idea, a perception. If your perception of yourself and your abilities are misconstrued, it's hard to see how you can break the "glass ceiling." This is a paradigm shift of action and philosophy. We need to understand that it takes our network of friends and peers to make it happen effectively.

We know women to be leaders in the community, at work, and exceptional mothers at home. Although in small numbers, we occupy everything from the C-Suites to board seats, including running our own businesses. We still have challenges: being accepted, receiving equal pay and equal rights, balancing work and home life, as well as being true to ourselves. How do we survive? We are Mother, Wife, Sister, Significant Other, Daughter, VP, CEO, Manager, Supervisor-- and our most beloved title, Friend. Even with the advancement of women, we still face untold social challenges. Could it be because we are just overwhelmed? According to a recent list based on the Fortune 1000 list of companies published by Fortune Magazine, women currently hold 4.8 percent of Fortune 500 CEO positions and 5.2 percent of Fortune 1000 CEO positions. What is holding us back from advancing ourselves further?

In business we tend to treat women who have obtained a managerial level or above with a certain hands-off approach. Leaving them alone to figure out the lay of the land by themselves. "She's got it" or "She can handle it," people tend to say regularly.

"Look at her, she's successful and has everything together." Really, what she needs is a support system, a small group of people who truly understand her plight. She needs peers who realize that although she may be strong, clever and assertive, sometimes she needs a mentor, advisor or trusted friend to turn to when in need of support and guidance.

Yes indeed, this mastermind conference for women would be powerful. It was quite clear that there were many issues we would need to address. The one thing we had to figure out was how to make these oh so powerful women open up and talk about what trials they were facing, so the masterminding could begin.

Then we thought, "How many times have we been to a conference and felt that we got nothing from it?" Kim and I could not allow this to happen. Pink Power had to be the difference that women were seeking, the answer to some of the challenges we face. Just like any plan, we had to have action steps and goals in place. The end result in mind had to forever stay in our minds: the promotion of masterminding amongst women. The take-away for the attendees would be a new platform for collaborative thinking, where women empowered each other with information and economic opportunity. They would have the ability to make solid connections and share their talents in a way that opened up opportunities for them all. Pink Power would represent a phenomenal group of women that would build opportunities and inspire growth.

In order to achieve this audacious goal, the next step was to develop content and topics that mattered to professional women. We both agreed that the days of hour-long speakers were long gone. Now people wanted real take-aways and nuggets of information they could instantly put to good use. Attention spans begin dwindling after 20 minutes. We discussed the idea of having "Pink Talks," short 10-15 minute talks given by a female expert in her field. We wanted our audience to remain excited and in anticipation of the next speaker. Agreeing that each attendee's experience had to be one they would never forget. I went out and began to share our vision and gain support for the conference. Organizations began to lend their support, speakers began to align their message, and most of all, other women began to get excited with the anticipation of something greater.

Pink Power: A MasterMind Conference For Women is now on to its way to a second conference. The magnitude of bringing career and businesswomen together is still being felt amongst each of us who were in attendance. What Kim and I envisioned came to fruition in the form of a movement. When there is need for positive change and a real vision, people will follow. Kim and I witnessed the power of pink, the ability to master your mind and to rise above and become true visionaries with the passion to ignite change for women globally.

About the Author

Felicia Phillips

Felicia Phillips is Managing Partner of Fillips International, Inc. an Atlanta based sustainability consulting and training firm. Fillips International assists businesses with establishing the framework for their sustainable initiatives. Fillips International has assisted in business development, asset recovery, electronic recycling and environmental awareness.

Ms. Phillips is the publisher of The Eco Review Magazine, an environmental magazine and the Visionary behind the Green Business Conference & Expo and Co-Founder of Pink Power: A MasterMind Conference for Women. In April 2011, Felicia was awarded the Phoenix Award by Mayor Kasim Reed for exemplary commitment to sustainability in the City of Atlanta. Felicia is currently the Co-Chair for the US-29 Eco Corridor in South Fulton.

As an environmental activist and motivational speaker her

topics include, Not My Son: Overcoming Autism, Building A Green Economy, Mainstreaming Sustainability, Living Green: What's In it for Me?, and other topics. She regularly participates on panels and has been a speaker for the Environmental Protection Agency, Women's Employment Opportunity Project, International Women's Think Tank, Georgia State University's Andrew Young School of Policy, Urban League of Greater Atlanta's Entrepreneurship Center, Fulton County Economic Development and other organizations.

Visit www.feliciaphillips.com for more information.

Reframing Failure with Success
Dr. Toni G. Alvarado

Failure is germane to every walk of life, social strata, family structure, ethnicity, and gender. Life has a way of happening to everyone. Much of what we experience can be completely out of our control. Sometimes failures are the result of our own negligence and/or malevolent behavior. In either case, whether failure is the result of our own doing, or catalyzed by the hand of another, failure is an aspect of life that all people will experience.

I enjoy reading biographies. I am fascinated by reading about the lives and experiences of historical figures. In many biographies the history and stories of people we hold in high esteem is retold in stunning detail. I am particularly intrigued by the success stories of those who report having overcome tragedies of loss and failure on their journey or road to success. Sam Chand, a contemporary leadership guru, states, "Most of our life experiences can be summed up as successes or failures. Few qualify as neutral incidents. Our society, families, churches, educational institutions, and mentors instruct us on the secrets of success, but not many gives us insights on successful failure."[1] The purpose of this chapter is to facilitate a paradigm shift for

---

1 Chand, Samuel R. Failure, *The Womb of Success* (Enumclaw, WA: WinePress Publishing, 1999) 21.

you on the topic of failure and its relationship to success. Failure is a Necessary Ingredient in The Recipe for Success. Failure is common to life. I have discovered that it is in fact a necessary ingredient in the recipe for success. Many people are comfortable talking about their successes and displaying their trophies, but few speak of failures as components of their success. I believe failure is one of the essential ingredients in the success recipe. For example, my first attempt at college was a dispiriting failure that became my motivation for future academic success. Without failure, success would be bland. Success devoid of failure would lack the rich wisdom that often accompanies the success we experience on the other side of failure.

Think of the joy you feel after a day of working diligently to complete a task. There is often an overwhelming sense of accomplishment. We even gain a sense of self-worth from an honest day's work. Success without failure is tantamount to accomplishment without hard work. Much like the feeling of satisfaction we feel when we have worked hard and accomplished our goals, there is an awe-inspiring sense of joy and satisfaction when we achieve a level of success after learning the lessons of failure.

How We Respond to Failure Often Determines Our Level of Success

Life is a series of happenings, some good, and some bad. Some experiences overwhelm us with unexpected joy while other experiences leave us emotionally drained, depleted, and exhausted. In actuality everyone desires to be successful in business, relationships, financially, and even physically, but much of our success is a direct correlation to how we handle failure. Using the Pareto Principle (20/80 Rule)[2], I have discovered that life is 20% what happens to us and 80% how we respond to it. As we survey the landscape of our lives, more than likely we can link our successes to corresponding momentary failures. I believe what makes success sweet is the bitterness of failure.

I'm thinking right now about the day George died. George was the 103 year old nursing home patient that I wrote about in my first book, *Run and Not Be Weary: The Pursuit of Purpose and Destiny.* I owe George much credit, for it was George who helped me figure out I had wasted 3 years of my life floundering around in nursing school, only to discover I was not suited for the profession. Growing up, I had two primary female role models. My grandmother was a devoted mother, grandmother, and housewife. She never worked outside of the home and only achieved a third grade education. My other role model was my own mother who had successfully completed nursing school and subsequently enjoyed a fruitful nursing career. Following my mother's example, after high school I enrolled in college to study nursing. Below is my first real encounter with failure that became the inspiration for my first book:

In general most people consider college to be a good thing, and nursing to be an honorable profession. Nursing was wonderful for my mother, but it was very wrong for me. God used the death of a 103-year old patent named George to compel me to finally acknowledge what I had secretly known throughout my nursing studies. George died during one of my clinical sessions as a nursing student.

2Maxwell, John C. *Developing the Leader With You.* (Nashville, TN: Thomas Nelson, Inc., 1993) 20-22.

Utterly overwhelmed and distressed by the task of preparing his body for the funeral home, I was forced to admit that I was obviously a very poor candidate for the nursing field. Could you imagine a nurse who is afraid of needles, blood and the dead? After three frustrating years as a nursing student, I withdrew from college.[3]

I left that experience feeling like a complete failure. It affected my self-esteem and confidence as it related to education and career options. Nearly a decade passed before I enrolled in college again. It was George that helped me figure out that I was not called to be a nurse. That revelation was a turning point for me. It wasn't until many years later that I gained the courage to face my failure and my fears. I went back to school and today I have 5 earned degrees, with over twenty years as a pastor, teacher, speaker, coach, and businesswoman.

Devastating Failures Are Just Another Stop on the Road to Success.

While I appreciate my own journey to success, my story is not much different than other successful people. History records many people who seemingly failed their first attempt at something great. Consider the below list of people whom we deem as successful today. This is not an exhaustive list of the world's greatest success stories. It is an abridged sample of athletes, entertainers, military leaders, political leaders, scientists, businessmen and womenwho experienced massive failure that could have easily caused

3 Alvarado, T. (2003). Run and Not Be Weary: The Pursuit of Purpose and Destiny. Grace House Ministries. 37-38.

them to give up on success. What they didn't know at the time was their monumental success would be a source of encouragement for all who watched them fail before they became successful and an impetus for my thesis that failure can be reframed when we continue on the journey of success. [4]

- Winston Churchill failed the 6th grade. He was defeated in every public office he ran for, before becoming the British Prime Minister at the age of 62.

- Thomas Edison's teachers told him he was "too stupid" to learn. It is said that he created 1000 light bulbs before creating the one that worked.

- Harland David Sanders, the famous "KFC Colonel," couldn't sell his chicken recipe. More than 1000 restaurants rejected his recipe for chicken and now there are KFC restaurants all over the world bearing his image.

- Mr. R.H. Macy had a history of failing businesses, including what was characterized as a dud Macy's store in New York City. Mr. Macy kept up his hard work and ended up with the biggest department store in the world! I would say that the department store in New York City couldn't be described as "dud" anymore.

- Steven Spielberg was rejected from his dream school, the University of California, three times. He sought education elsewhere and dropped out to be a movie director.

4 "23 Successful People Who Failed At First" (2014, March). Retrieved from http://www.businessinsider.com/successful-people-who-failed-at-first

- Mr. Soichiro Honda was passed over for an engineering job at Toyota and left unemployed until he started manufacturing motorcycles. I would say he has been pretty successful seeing that Honda is now a multi-billion dollar business and a major manufacturer of cars around the world.

- Vera Wang failed to make the U.S. Olympic figure skating team. She later became an editor at Vogue magazine and was passed over for the editor-in-chief position. She began designing wedding gowns at the age of 40 and today she is one of the premier designers in the wedding industry with a multi-billion dollar business.

- Walt Disney was fired as a newspaper editor because he "lacked imagination" and had no good ideas.

- The first time Jerry Seinfeld went onstage he was booed by jeering crowds.

- After Sydney Poitier's first audition, the casting director instructed him to just stop wasting everyone's time and "go become a dishwasher or something else."

- Oprah Winfrey was fired from her first television job because they told her she wasn't fit to be on the screen.

- Lucille Ball spent many years on the B-list and her agent told her to pursue a new career.

- 27 different publishers rejected Dr. Seuss' first book.

- Henry Ford's Motor Company filed bankruptcy twice

before he became successful in his third attempt.

- Steve Jobs was fired from the company he started. He was later hired back and experienced incredible success.

As you can probably see from this list of people who changed the world despite their failures, devastating failures are just another stop on the road to success.

Reframing Failure

Reframing is a cognitive method of changing the meaning of something and thereby changing the mindset about an experience. Reframing is a communication tool used in neurolinguistic programming, negotiation therapy, public relations, and many other fields. Cognitive reframing is a psychological technique that counteracts irrational and maladaptive thoughts. Reframing is best used to dispel negative thoughts about past experiences.

Whether the failure we experience is related to business, career, education, or relationships, self-defeating thoughts and self-limiting beliefs can arise. These negative thoughts often cause us to believe we are not good enough or do not deserve to be successful. The danger of embracing self-limiting beliefs is that these types of thoughts prevent us from realizing our full potential. Reframing is a learned skill that counteracts self-limiting beliefs with positive thoughts. This weakens negative self-concepts and increases our ability to achieve immeasurable success.

Think of reframing as new software that must be downloaded into your brain that erases negative thoughts and feelings about past failures. It is a matter of perspective. Reframing allows us to reprogram our perspective on life's experiences and causes us to see the good in every situation. When I reframe my thoughts on an experience, I see positivity where I once saw negativity. I see gain where I once saw loss. I see an opportunity where I once saw a challenge. Finally, I see a lesson learned that could be used as a skill in my present and future success.

The question remains, "How does one reframe failure with success?" Here is what I have surmised from my own life and the experiences of other successful people. Consider these suggestions and apply this wisdom to your life for a successful future.

Keep Moving Forward

Don't allow past failure to paralyze you. What do you think would have happened if the successful people named on the previous pages allowed past failures to stifle them? The world would be devoid of many witty inventions we now enjoy. Had those persons not persevered through failure, we would lack much of the wisdom that came from their failures.

Whenever I am coaching people who are rebounding from past disappointments and mistakes, I use the analogy of lessons learned from the design of automobiles. I assist my clients in recognizing the reasons why the windshield is bigger than the rear view mirror of a car. The windshield and rear view mirror are both important parts of any vehicle. They each serve a particular purpose and both are vital to the operation of the automobile.

The windshield serves as a protector from the weather and even a projectile shield in the event of an automobile accident. The rear view mirror of a vehicle is equally vital for protection. It provides drivers with a view of the area behind them. Many modern automobiles are built with rear view cameras that are activated when the car is placed in the reverse gear. However, there is a disclaimer on most rear view mirrors and cameras that warns drivers that the pictures can be a distorted view of the area behind the vehicle.

The windshield allows the driver to see the road that leads to the desired destination. The windshield of a car is wide and clear allowing the driver to see far ahead, viewing the markers and signs that indicate their progress and the closeness of the destination. The windshield protects the driver and passengers from debris that is hurled at the vehicle while progressing toward its destination.

The rear view mirror is important because it helps us to gauge the closeness of the approaching traffic. The rear view mirror informs us how far we have traveled. This is often a source of encouragement for the weary traveler who has become discouraged on the journey. Yet, if we are preoccupied with the objects in the rear view mirror we become distracted and increase the potential for accidents and mishaps.

Past failure is much like an object in the rear view mirror. It is distorted reality. We cannot deny that we have failed. However, if we are not careful, past failure will convince us that it is "closer than it appears." Focusing on our failure can lead us to believe that we will never move past it. The windshield of every vehicle is larger than the rearview mirror because where we are going is more important than where we have been! So, keep moving forward.

Stay Focused

Don't allow past failure to distract you. Distraction comes in many forms. We can become preoccupied with our own failure and the failures of others. It is human nature to experience feelings of remorse, sorrow, and guilt whenever we fail. While we need to peer into the rear view mirror at particular junctures, if we focus more on the rear view mirror than the windshield we can become distracted, causing us to miss important indicators that tell us to when to slow down, stop, change lanes, turn, exit the highway or worse, cause an accident.

Focus is required if we are to achieve success. Successful people are not easily distracted. They are single-minded like a marathon runner. Successful people keep their eyes on the prize. If we allow the pain of past failures to distract us, it is likely that we will be pulled into reverse. Instead of moving ahead we will be moving backwards, remaining stuck in old patterns of behavior. Distracted thinking has the potential to sabotage new opportunities for success. Reframing failure by staying focused is a skill that can be compared to looking intently through the windshield of an automobile while driving. The span and clarity of the windshield represents forward thinking. Focused thoughts and actions have the potential to lead you to limitless possibilities and successes.

Remain Optimistic

Optimism is the attitude of expectation for favorable change. It is the skill of finding the silver lining behind every cloud. Forward motion in life requires optimistism. Do not allow failure to define or confine you to a current moment or past experience in your life. An optimistic person is one who predicts the best possible, realistic outcome from every negative experience. Reframing failure with success requires optimism and optimism is a matter of perspective.

Psychological and medical research reveals that optimism has positive effects on the body and mind. Researchers have discovered that optimists handle the stress of failure more healthily than pessimists. D. Goleman discovered that when optimists encounter disappointment such as not getting a job, or not being promoted on their current job, they are more focused on what they can do to improve their situation, rather than dwelling on their frustrations or on the things they cannot change.[5]

Recent research from the Mayo Clinic reveals a number of health benefits associated with optimism.[6] So powerful is positive thinking that researchers S. Segerstrom and S. Sephton linked optimism to a healthy immune system. They discovered that people who were optimistic about negative experiences exhibited a stronger immune response and were even more successful in school than those who had a negative view on their experiences.[7] They further report that increased activity in areas of the brain associated with negative emotions lead to a weaker immune system and mades a person more susceptible to viruses.[8] According to the Mayo Clinic and other medical scientists, optimism

5 Goleman, D. (1987). Research affirms power of positive thinking. New York Times. Found online at http://psychology.about.com/od/PositivePsychology/a/benefits-of-positive-thinking.htm
6 Mayo Clinic. (2011). Positive thinking: Reduce stress by limiting negative self-talk. Found online at http://psychology.about.com/od/PositivePsychology/a/benefits-of-positive-thinking.htm
7 Segrestrom S. and Sephton S. (2010). Optimistic expectancies and cell-mediated immunity: The role of positive affect. Psychological Science, 21 (3), 448-55.
8 Ibid. 448-55.

reduces the risk of death associated with cardiovascular problems, decreases depression, improves the immune system, and results in an overall increase in life span.

Have you ever wondered how two people can have the same experience and one person comes away with a positive outlook while the other person comes away with a negative or pessimistic demeanor? Reframing is a cognitive tool that allows one to choose the frame you place around your thoughts about failure. You can remain optimistic and view the glass half full, or you can be pessimistic to view the glass half empty. It is your choice. Choose the right frame, remain optimistic, and increase your chances for success.

Glean Wisdom from Failure

Your past failure is not indicative of your future potential for success. In fact, many successful leaders candidly share that they have gained more wisdom from their failure than from their success. In their book, *The Wisdom of Failure*, Laurence G. Weinzimmer and Jim McConoughey suggest that we can only succeed by knowing failure. This paradoxical statement is proven in the comparison they make in their profiles of such leaders as Ken Lay, former Chair and CEO of Enron – the key figure of the highly publicized Enron scandal and Jim Owens, former CEO of Caterpillar, Inc.

Weinzimmer and McConoughey report from the Harvard Business Review interview of A.G. Lafley, former CEO of Proctor and Gamble who answered the question, "Can leaders learn as much from success as they do from failure?" In answering this question, A.G. Lafley, responded, "No. My experience is that we learn much more from failure than we do from success." Lafley refers to his failure as "gifts" because of the tremendous growth he experienced as a leader from his failures.

Only when you learn the lessons of failure can you genuinely offer insights and wisdom to those coming behind you. Consider these quotes from men and women who have gleaned wisdom from failure:

- "If you accept failure as an opportunity to learn, it will change your whole perspective." Catherine Pulsifer

- "A failure is a man who has blundered but is not capable of cashing in on the experience." Elbert Hubbard

- "Courage is going from failure to failure without losing enthusiasm." Winston Churchill

- "Experience is simply the name we give our mistakes." Oscar Wilde

- "Good people are good because they've come to wisdom

  through failure. We get very little wisdom from success, you know." William Saroyan

- "I don't believe in failure. It's not failure if you enjoyed the process." Oprah Winfrey

- "I have not failed. I've just found 10,000 ways that won't work." Thomas Edison

- "I've missed more than 9000 shots in my career. I've lost more than 300 games. 26 times I've been trusted to take the game winning shot and missed. I've failed over and over and over again in my life and that's why I succeed." Michael Jordan

- It is often failure who is the pioneer in new lands, new undertakings, and new forms of expression." Eric Hoffer

- "Failure is simply the opportunity to begin again only more intelligently." Henry Ford

- "Failure is filled with nuggets of wisdom that when gleaned and properly applied can result in immeasurable success." Dr. Toni G. Alvarado

Failure Is Not Final

The frame we choose to place around a painting can increase its beauty and value. Even a cheap painting can be upgraded to a beautiful piece of art when it is reframed with the right material. Reframing failure does not mean we do not take responsibility for our past mistakes. In fact, when a painter paints a picture and frames it, one of the last things she does is sign the painting. Her signature indicates that she owns the painting, its merits and its flaws. Reframing failure is simply an attitude that refuses to accept failure as final.

What is success? Albert Einstein once said, "Try not to become a success, but rather to be of value." Most people think of their value in relation to business and financial wealth. Yet, true success cannot be measured in material possessions and monetary value. Success is measured by our ability to respond to failure with a positive attitude that improves our character, strengthens our weaknesses, and gains us wisdom found only on the other side of failure. If we think of failure as something from which we can never rebound, we will be forever tied to an experience that was designed to teach us the true meaning of success. ***"Failure is not final. It depends on how you frame it!"***

Visit www.drtonialvarado.com for more information.

About the Author

Dr. Toni G. Alvarado

Dr. Toni G. Alvarado is the Chief Executive Officer of My Sister's Keeper Foundation for Women a leading influential organization focused on "Moving Women from Average to Excellence" in their educational, personal and professional development and pursuits. She is a Certified Professional Coach & Coach Trainer with over 20 years of success as a wife, mother, entrepreneur and the President of Targeted Living Coaching & Consulting, LLC.

Dr. Toni is the Co-Pastor of Grace Church International and Adjunct Professor at Beulah Heights University in Atlanta, GA. She is the author of Run and Not Be Weary: The Pursuit of Purpose and Destiny. She co-authored Let's Stay Together: Relationship Strategies For Successful Marriages, with her husband Dr. Johnathan E. Alvarado.

Dr. Toni's Coaching Niche's are: Women in Ministry,

Business and Corporate Leadership, Work/Life Balance, Educational and Professional Goal/Planning, Self-Care and Healthy Relationships. She is passionate about fitness training, reading, writing and spending time with her husband and three children. Her years of experience as a community leader, pastor, professor, coach and trainer coupled with her educational accomplishments imminently qualify her to empower others.

Success Sharpens Success
Mentors, Friends and Life Coaches
Robin White

Have you ever noticed that successful people are always talking about having mentors and coaches? There's proof to having accountability partners and coaches that help you climb the success ladder. Coaches help you see things that you're not able to see for yourself. For example, in my experience with sports, my coaches knew my strengths, and they knew how to help me overcome my weaknesses. They motivated me to surpass heights I never knew I could reach. We achieve milestones we doubted to our own abilities and mindsets.

When I work with clients, as a life and executive coach, I find out their goals and visions. Our abilities and mindsets are the keys to achieving goals that we once considered impossible! We then build a plan to make them a reality. In my 13 years of consulting and speaking I have seen many people who don't even know what they want or how to accomplish it. I think that many people live life without goals, they strive for. They just accept how life is, and consider mediocrity as something that's meant to be. It's doubt and fear that motivates such thinking. We all feel doubtful, but we can't buy into it. The ones who buy into the failure, fear or doubt one day find themselves in a rut and cannot get out of it. When in doubt, have faith and trust progress.

When I ask what their definition of success is, many of them admit to not having one. The good news is though, if you're feeling the same way, that's completely normal. However, you can be in a rut, or you can build a success plan and begin living your life the way it was intended for you. Begin focusing on what would satisfy you. So many people ask the same questions: "How do you do it?" "How do you achieve success?," "What if I don't know what will make me happy?" It takes a bit of searching. Doubt shouldn't prevent you from becoming successful. You must have trust, faith, and the right people around you. More faith becomes more action. Start with the tips below:

Action tip 1 - Find your definition of what success means to you. Is it having a degree, your own business, family, children, a spouse or a career that you love and feel successful working in? If time, energy and money were not an issue what would you do?

Action tip 2 - Surround yourself with people who see your vision and support both you and your new endeavor, people who will hold you accountable. Do you! Be alive and positive. People love to be around positive, successful people.

Action tip 3 - Do it! Work on the plan day by day. Understand that focus and intentions are important. Don't let distractions take away your concentration on what you want for your life. Know your professional and personal plan. Get a mentor or a life coach to help you find your success, What's your vision?

What would make you feel satisfied? Keep in mind, some of those goals may take days, months, even years, but you'll be on the right track.

Be BOLD

After creating your plan of attack for success, you will then need to improve your communication skills. It's an acquired skill that can improve with the desire to be better. If you want to find your success you have to research, ask questions, gather information, and build relationships. In order to do that you must improve your verbal, non-verbal, and written skills of communication. Many times we are taught that we need job security, but when we look at it from a point of view of success, it should be skill security. If you have skills, you have the confidence to communicate your needs. You can then choose whatever career you want.

Do you ever wonder why some people connect with people in a quick second and others struggle to find the right words to say? It isn't always personality traits and comfort level. Some of the most confident people are also nervous and uncomfortable, but they realize it is part of the overall picture of success. They also work on their communication skills constantly. I teach workshops around the world and have to laugh when I see that people do not like when conference or seminar leaders ask the participants to network with each other, because many struggle with it or hate doing it. Where else can you practice a skill set in a safe place?

Also, be careful in a professional setting that we can become "gabby" or "chatty" about the wrong things. Professionals don't discuss personal issues or negative conversations with people they do not know. Please take note of that. One you can come across like a loose cannon and two, they really don't care about your ailments and personal issues. They may act concerned or empathetic, but I can promise you they are judging your choice of conversation. Many times it will come back later to bite you. Conversations should consist of the industry and light hearted topics. Happy people love being around other happy people. The old rule that politics, religion, and sex are topics that shouldn't be discussed is still relevant to business conversations. This rule also applies to written communication, such as on social media, texting, and emailing also includes rules in your written communication skills, whether emails, texting or even resumes. Some people may think we have changed as a society in our communications with texting and social media, etc. Keep in mind that there are still professionals who will make a mental note if they see you texting in a meeting, or in front of others in a professional setting. They will also make notes if they see behavior on social media sites that is unprofessional. It can be a double standard, but do yourself a favor and don't do it if you want to make an incredible impression. As I meet many managers and business owners that do the hiring for their companies, they mention that they always check references and social media behavior. After all, they want someone who portrays a positive image for their company.

We should be confident and professional in how we introduce ourselves; first impressions are important. I like to refer to this introduction as the 'toot your horn' speech. Most people in your company probably know how to give their professional introduction. I will include that in the action tips. Practice and perfect it!

Action tip 1: Evaluate your communications skills

Do your words match my actions? Do you speak without thinking? Do you let your emotions control you? Do you hold a grudge? Do you jump to conclusions? Are you absolutely clear in your communication? Are you a confident communicator? When you introduce yourself is your body language sending a good message? Make sure you are aware of these communication signals that could be hurting you.

Action tip 2- Can you communicate with all types of people

Differences in culture, ethnic backgrounds, geography, lifestyle, age, gender, education, economic standing, technology, understanding of social media require different sets of communication skills. for example: The accounting department to the Sales department to the VP and the CEO! Get involved in diverse groups. Be a sponge and a learner.

Action tip 3-Improve your networking and professional communication image

Are you able to connect with people and promote yourself without being uncomfortable? Do you have a 'toot your horn' speech? Here is a quick template:

Begin with...

I am_____ (name and title)
for_____ (company name)
I do ____ (what your duties are)
so that _____(mention your value and assets to the company here)

Here is a sample to help you see and work on your own.

"I am Robin White. I am a motivational speaker, published author and life coach for MOTV8U LLC. I light a fire in the belly of people who want to see their vision, reach their goals so that they can live a successful life of happiness, and understand their purpose."

This last part "so that" is truly important. It is the selling point of what is in it for them. Most of us as women don't like to sound arrogant or cocky so we don't know how to address the value of what we do. Most down play their importance in a company role. One of my favorite speakers and dear friends, Dr. Angela Massey teaches audiences of women to "Kill the Justa".

What does it mean? Have you ever met a doctor, or an attorney and they say "I'm *justa* doctor? I'm *justa* lawyer? Own who you are and bring confidence to the table. Why would I want to do business with someone who thinks they are "justa receptionist," "justa accountant," "justa mom." Ladies, stop the madness. OWN IT! Be BOLD

Be Beautiful

In my career as a motivational speaker, I've spoken in front of thousands of people in different venues, arenas, and conferences all over the world. I am often asked, "Do you get nervous?" My answer is NO! When I enter a room, conference or workshop I own the room and am blessed and grateful to have an opportunity to change people's lives.

It's my calling. I have found my passion and I enjoy it.

I don't think of it as being nervous. It's energy, excitement from adrenaline. The only time I have gotten a little nervous is when I speak in front of my peers. I know my peers that are reading this book can probably relate; there's something about the adrenaline of speaking in front of your peers that makes you just a little bit more anxious. Stand tall, with your head straight, and speak clearly and intelligently. Most importantly, be you. My hope is for you to find your passion. When you love what you do, you don't work a day in your life. When we successfully do something we love our confidence levels are always higher. What do you love to do? Are you doing what you love? Why not? Check yourself from time to time, in a meeting, at a social event, one-on-one with a co-worker or a boss: am I speaking confidently or am I trying to disappear?

Your esteem is your own responsibility. No one will give you the energy you need to feel strong and confident but yourself. You are 100 % responsible for this. Don't blame it on parents, coaches, friends, teachers, or others. Do these folks have a huge impact on your esteem? Of course! However, no one has the impact on your esteem more than you do. It is a daily chore. We brush our teeth, make our beds, and do daily chores. We should include saying self-affirmations and having positive conversations with yourself.

One of my favorite mentors and greatest motivational speakers out there today is Jack Canfield. I've read all of his material and quote him frequently in my conferences. One of my favorite concepts he speaks on is his poker chip theory. Enjoy his concept, but apply it daily.

"Jack's Poker Chip Theory of Success"

In Las Vegas, you see people at the table who are making $20,000 bets and others making $5 bets. If I'm making $5 bets, I don't lose as much but I can never win as much as higher betters do. Our self-esteem is like poker chips. If you have a lot of poker chips, you're going to play much more freely than if you only had 5 instead of 100. I'm going to lose one bet of 5 and I'm out of the game forever.

You lose two bets of 5 and you've still got 90 chips left.

To be successful, it's important for people to build up their self-esteem and their confidence, partially by having successes–which build up your confidence–but also by taking care of your psychological functions. Most people don't even realize they have these functions and that they're responsible for controlling and maintaining the highest level of self-confidence. It begins today just start saying "today I'm going to start being beautiful, confident, successful" whatever it is that you want you have to just begin saying it. Make it your focus and your intention and that starts now.

I had a client approach me and say that her daughter was struggling with low self-esteem and confidence. She wanted to know how to help her and support her. She didn't know what to say to her.

I asked her, "How is your self-esteem?"

She looked at me with this look of confusion and I replied,"Honey, you can't teach something you don't have!"

As mothers and daughters, we want to have high self-esteem, but we use other people's opinions to judge us and we believe them. In my book, *Fat Girls Don't Eat French Fries,*

I teach how to overcome our previous experiences to help us move forward and not stay stuck in the past. Being beautiful and loving life regardless of our circumstances. Get started:

Action tip 1- Get out of your comfort zone. You learn more about you and your character when uncomfortable. Work on confidence daily. Do it! Start today! Believe in yourself! Don't worry about what others want for you. What do you want for you? Be ok with being uncomfortable.

Action tip 2 - Be your biggest cheerleader. Be beautiful. Be unique. Be happy. Is it sabotage? Is it fear of success? The unknown? What is the worst thing that can happen? What is the best? Own your strengths. Don't beat yourself up over your weaknesses. Start today by building your poker chip pile.

Action tip 3 - Work on happiness daily. What does that look like and feel like? How do you talk to yourself? Are you overly critical or confident? Are you pushing yourself to be your best? What is your desire and how are you working toward that daily? Do you write down your goals and vision plan of what happy would look like or feel like. Focus on those plans daily.

Be YOU

So OWN IT GIRL. No matter what shape, size, age, whatever you have been given, it is a gift. You need to see it that way.

Most women who are between the ages of 40-60 years of age say they begin to really love their bodies at this age. They feel more freedom, less pressure, and more confident. Why can't we learn this as young women? I believe when we are young we put pressure on ourselves to compete. Let's help these beautiful young women not waste 20, 30 years and maybe even a lifetime. Stop lying to yourselves. Most people have a lot of fears. We are always living in fear, the fear of success, the fear of the unknown, the fear of looking dumb, the fear of moving forward, etc. What are we so afraid of? I have a hard time answering this one myself. Some days are better than others. Sometimes I look in the mirror and say to myself, "It just isn't going to happen today." My mother used to say to me that you have to appreciate the bad days too. She also taught me to not go out of the house without fresh makeup, a decent outfit, and your hair done nicely. That was a true indication of self-respect and keeping up with appearances. When you look good you feel good. When you feel good you carry yourself well.

That brings me to my next point. To be you it is imperative that you have the right people around you. Ones that will keep you honest, humble, that will pick you up when you need, laugh when you need, and cry with you, when you need, to! We need a supportive system around us. Having negative friends and family can bring us down. Whether you hang out with church friends, school friends, professionals or long-term friends, you have to be true to yourself and honest with them.

Sometimes people are placed in our path for a certain amount of time for a specific reason. We may never know the reason, but take a good look at the relationship you have with this person and ask yourself if it is healthy. If not let it go. It may be hard to do, but you cannot grow as a woman if you are hanging on to old baggage. It will bring you down. You may not see it at first but once you let it go and reflect back, you will kick yourself and ask "Why didn't I do that earlier?"

This may be with friends, relationships and even jobs. If you are like me, you've have had people talk about you behind your back, but smile in your face. These are behaviors of immature people, don't buy into it. It is your responsibility to control your surroundings. Be direct and honest with people about how you need them to support you in your journey as a secure, confident person.

Find a job that works for you, that showcases your talents and helps you conquer fears and challenges. We gain confidence by doing things we love. When we do something great it makes us feel great. So if you are working a boring job that doesn't build your talents then you're probably not moving forward. How many days do you wake up, mumbling to yourself on the way to the shower, I hate this job, this day is going to be long and boring? If those thoughts are running through your mind in the morning they are probably running through your mind all day. This contributes to negative thoughts and low self-esteem.

Women tend to analyze and over analyze so these thoughts don't just go away. If we consistently ponder and think about negative things in our life, what do you think this will ultimately do to your health and wellness? Not to mention self-esteem.

Think about the time you spend at work, and then add the number of days, months and years. Add all the time up and consider the amount of time you spend not feeling good. It becomes you. That is your life and the choices that you are making in your life.

Look at the negative people in your life. Why do we allow them to be so negative? Studies show that on average we hear 300 negative comments a day and only 20 positive things a day.

Let's change that as strong confident women. Start building each other up and holding each other accountable. This is my one major wish for women to see how powerful it can be to be successful together. You can change your own mind and change the perspective of our society. We are not to compare ourselves to anyone else on this planet. Our frame, our weight, our looks are all unique to us. When we begin to realize this truth, the thought cycle of superficiality begins to disappear.

Women who compare themselves to Hollywood stars are setting themselves up for an unrealistic goal. These stars have issues and problems of their own that we fail to acknowledge. We see what we want to see in them. Fancy clothes, diamonds, money, partying, lots of attention. But are any of those people happy? The ones that are, are the ones who don't fall into the paparazzi trap or the tabloids. They love themselves and their families. They are stable and it's because they have made the effort to do so. Look at the ones who are happy. They are blessed in their own skin. So start now, who can you help to be strong, confident and successful? Success sharpens success and you can be part of the change. Begin with you!

Action tip 1- Start being honest. What is it really that you are afraid of? Stay consistent with good behaviors. Reward yourself when you feel you need to. It is very important to not deprive yourself and feel proud of your hard work.

Action tip 2 - Most importantly, change your thoughts and perceptions in your mind. What has happened to you in the past is now over. Move through it and focus your attention on what you want to achieve, not what you haven't.

Action tip 3 - Be YOU. Be confident in your own skin and begin to be a better you. Help other women see the power of change. After all, we are in this together. Successful people hang out with successful people. Which one are you?

About the Author

Robin White

With nonstop energy and infectious enthusiasm, Robin White instantly builds rapport with audiences whenever she speaks. She is a natural and dynamic presenter, trainer, and professional developer. Always entertaining, Robin drives home key points in her training with fascinating anecdotes and stories from her many travels around the world as an international speaker and educator. Robin's training sessions often include small-group exercises that engage the audience and make remembering important points easier. Wherever she presents, she is a breath of fresh air for participants and easily becomes a workplace favorite. Audiences always come away with techniques and practical tools they can put to use immediately to be more effective in their jobs. Whatever your workplace training needs, Robin White has the expertise to address them. She also possesses a personal flair that will make her presentation a standout from any seminar, retreat, or company presentation your employees have ever encountered before. She's the "real deal" and a speaker your employees will enjoy and remember always!

Be Bold
Be Beautiful
Be You.

MOTV8U LLC
Author of "Fat Girls Don't Eat French Fries"
www.motv8ullc.com
motv8u1 - Twitter
motv8u1 - YouTube

Finding the Way Back to Myself
Tia Buckham-White

Have you ever been in a situation where you realized you were the problem you've always been complaining about? Have you reached that epiphany, that "self-actualization" stuff psychologists are always rambling on about, where everything becomes, clear as glass? In this moment you discover your own responsibility in why things have repeatedly taken the same turn in your life. This first happened to me about 14 years ago.

Let me start at the beginning. My husband and I were taking care of my father-in-law, who was in the early stages of Dementia/Alzheimer's, and we were struggling in our relationship. We decided to go to a therapist, and this is where my journey began. I am not promoting a specific way to understand yourself. I am only saying you can find your way in life when you least expect it or when you are not looking for it.

The therapist was nice and peaceful, but I did not feel like she could help us. As a professional, she did a lot of fishing for positive affirmation about her work. I didn't feel as if we connected with her and was aggravated by her approach. She told me that I had a "strong personality," which I'd heard before from people who were not African-American. I could not accept her feedback, nor did I agree with her perspective.

We found another therapist, an African-American male and Licensed Clinical Social Worker (LCSW). He required that in addition to our couple's therapy, we each attend a therapeutic men's group and women's group. The experience of working with this counselor was powerful and difficult at the same time. It began my process of understanding me, because others were empowered to tell me what they thought of my behavior. They told me the truth, but I did not want to accept it.

I was introduced to an experience that made me painfully aware of my involvement of what was happening to me as an individual, in my familial, work and friendship relations. This was an eye opener, and it caused me to think. Maybe what I was doing affected these relationships in a negative way and in order for those relationships to change, I needed to change my behavior. I began the path back to myself, even though I did not know I was lost. I slowly began to see who I was and how my demeanor impacted my relationships. This was difficult to receive at first. As I began to uncover and discover more things about my personality, I wanted to learn more and understand why I behaved in a particular way. I had to ask myself some really hard questions, such as, "Was I affecting the outcomes of my relationships and blaming them on other people?" I knew my marriage was struggling. I knew I was not where I wanted to be at work. I knew my familial relationships could use some help and I also knew my friendships could be a lot better.

How did I know it could be better? I knew because I was having struggles in all relational areas in my life. Initially, it did not occur to me that I was in discord on various levels in my life. My perspective had always been that each struggle was due to someone else's problem. Let me show you a few examples of this in my various relationships.

My Marriage

Fourteen years ago, my husband Michael and I were having deep in difficulties our marriage. I felt that the issue with his ailing father was difficult to deal with, and needed to be approached differently. Michael didn't agree with the way I thought he should handle the situation. Until this time in our relationship he never disagreed to this degree with me. Things changed once we started dealing with his father's illness. When problems arose in the past, we would argue a bit about it, but he would eventually come around and we would move forward with some type of agreement. But now when a situation arose, he didn't budge. I was not used to that, and the more he said no, the more aggressive and argumentative I became. In my mind, he should have listened to me. The unhappiness I was feeling was a result of him not listening to me and doing things in a way in which I totally disagreed. I never thought it had anything to do with me – because I always made it about him. In retrospect, this was such a damaging way to show up in a relationship, but I was consciously and unconsciously committed to my way of viewing the world.

My Career

I have always held decent jobs. I obtained a Broadcast Journalism Degree in 1993, but my first post-grad job was as a ticket agent for Delta Airlines. I had a great experience there, where I was exposed to the airline's proprietary software ticketing process. This job introduced me to the Information Technology (IT) field. I worked with various software systems such as IT recruiting and library. It was also my first time working in an environment where I was the only person of color and one of few a women. Conflict stalked me in the world of IT, and every difficult situation I encountered was, according to me, about someone else. If someone said something I didn't like, I'd assume they were questioning my abilities. If my target numbers were second best, I'd believe others were questioning my effort. I was unaware of how my thoughts led to my adverse reactions to others. Whenever I felt I was being second guessed, I would become defensive. As a result of my unconscious behavior, I created negative perceptions of myself with my work teams and completely fed into the stereotypes of both women and people of color. Despite all of that, though, in the late 90's I was able to land an excellent opportunity working with a corporation providing software training. In this environment I was part of a diverse and progressive team, but as you would have guessed, conflict followed me there as well.

My Family Relationships

I'm very close to my mother's side of the family; my cousins are like siblings. But even with that intimacy, I still engaged in major disagreements with the majority of them. I believe my younger cousins avoided connecting with me because of what they witnessed in my interactions with others. My mother and I clashed a lot during my college years. Our major point of contention was born when I found out that my biological father was not who I thought he was. This is another example of how I was not aware of my deeper feelings and how they showed up in my personal interactions. I believed the conflicts I was having with my family members was due to them trying to hurt me. Maybe it was because they were dealing with their own issues? Maybe…They were hurting just like me, and were coping just like me, and probably completely unaware of how they were contributing to the conflict, just like me. Regardless, whatever was going on with them was of no prime importance to me, because I believed that they did something to me and what I said or did was of no consequence, it was a result dealing with their failures in our relationship.

My Friendships

In college I altered my personality from high school to become more confident and open. I had multiple groups of friends, but I preferred hanging out with girls who knew more than me. When I spent time with some women in my age group, I experienced conflicts with them. I based the reasons for these conflicts on how I felt about each group, which I categorized by economic status or social status. At different times, I felt like an outsider when I was around them.

One friend especially worth mentioning would be my relationship with my roommate and her friends. I enjoyed being around them, but my roommate felt that at times I was off-putting. She would call me dramatic and always made me feel like I was offending her. I didn't see myself the way she did. Regardless, whatever was going on with her was of no prime importance, because I believed that it was her problem and not my mine.

Turning the Corner

Joining a therapeutic women's group helped me to see my flaws, as well as opportunities for change. Having a therapist focused on helping all of us women see ourselves and empower the group to give their honest opinion about their experiences with one another, made a difference in my understanding of myself. I began to see that my perspective on my relationships, whether personal or professional, had an effect on the outcomes of my interactions with others.

Having the therapist in my one-on-one sessions tell me the truth about how I was showing up behaviorally to him, the sessions with Michael, and the sessions with my group, gave me the first real understanding of what my responsibilities are to my relationships.

As I've stated previously, going through this process was very difficult for me. Receiving feedback about my behavior still confounded me, and I remained argumentative and unwilling to listen to others opinions. I believed a disagreement I had with anyone was always about the other person 'forcing' me to tell them off. This belief system was keeping me away from my real self. On another level, I now see that I was being my real self, even though that real self was confused, ignorant, sad, and scared and I absolutely did not believe that I was any of those things at the time.

Why wouldn't I believe that, you ask? Well, from a familial, cultural, and societal perspective I was taught being strong meant you spoke your mind and did not back down or yield. If you told someone off, it was because they made you do it. So I believed, consciously or not, that the discord in my life was caused by others. I was just doing what I had to do to survive.

I now understand this is as a dysfunctional way of seeing the world, but you could not have fully convinced me of this before I started going to people who could help me and asked God for personal insight. Due to my emotional life experience, it took me 10+ years to TRULY see this. When I look back over those years I realize the initial reason I went to talk with someone was to begin the journey of finding myself. It was me looking for my purpose. I needed all the experiences in my life to help me learn how to change my personal beliefs about relationships and receive honest feedback from people on how they experienced me. Beginning the process toward this way of thinking was a necessary part of my personal life path.

It was ultimately one group session that helped me to turn the corner. During this session, I overreacted to someone's response to me, because I perceived them as avoiding a question I asked. I unconsciously behaved aggressively by pushing them to answer my question. The therapist interjected and pointed out that I 'seemed' angry. My response was that I was not an angry, but that the person needed to answer the question. It was at that moment that I stood up to argue my point further. The therapist responded that I was acting as if I was angry. Of course I kept saying that I was not angry in an aggressive tone. The therapist calmly asked me if he needed to call the authorities to have me removed. I was dumbfounded and immediately calmed down.

The therapist asked the group to respond to my behavior. "Let's go around the room and have each person say how they experienced Tia." The reactions ranged from mortification to complete reverie, but all the answers, no matter how they were delivered, were consistent: they described me as angry, sad, scared, and intimidating. Hearing the feedback left me saddened, embarrassed, and confused. I realized later that deep inside of me, I knew they were telling the truth. I could no longer hide or blame anyone else. I finally saw and accepted who I was and made the decision to redirect and change my life.

One of the main reasons I was able to accept the feedback from the group was that these people didn't know me personally, and had no reason to lie to me. The more reserved people in the group would say they hated to state some things about my behavior, but they had to be honest with me. I felt that the more direct they were with me, the more they could also see themselves, and that helped them, too. The group interaction brought me to a level of self-awareness that set me on a path of healing. This self-discovery forced me to look at myself and wonder if I appeared to be angry and out of control to the other people in my life. This thought haunted me. It became my mission to be conscious about my demeanor in every public engagement with others. Not because I felt paranoid, but because I felt like I now had the key to successfully deal with people. I was in full control. Although I am nowhere near perfect, I am now more self-aware. When interacting with other people, I pay attention to body language and if I notice a shift, I modify my behavior immediately.

Now for example, in social situations, if a particular subject comes up and I start speaking about it and the person I am speaking with sits back, or starts looking at other people, or asks for others' perspectives. I manage that interaction much better. I yield or ask clarifying questions in a calm and confident way. It makes a difference in how I respond. In the past, the lack of clarity from the sender would confuse me and I would unconsciously become reactive to the nonverbal behavior.

My Mindset Shift

Changing your mindset and becoming more aware of how your behavior has influence over how others react to you is important to your personal and professional development. This perspective can create a new avenue of empowerment for communities worldwide. Personally, I was not aware of how I was coming across to people with whom I was trying to communicate. Since I had acted this way the majority of my adult life, I could not see past my own perspective. How many of us are unaware of the impact our behavior has over the way people react and deal with us? How many relationships have failed because of this? How many promotions have been missed? How many people feel unhappy about how they are engaging with the people in their lives, but feel powerless to change this problem? When you discover your authentic self, it is a great feeling. You will overcome your confusion and powerlessness and create better relationships with others.

Where I Am Today

Today I am in a different place. It is empowering to see yourself as others truly experience you; it is life changing. As a result of this experience, I have a much better marriage and my other relationships are amazing… amazing! The forward-thinking ideas of a great therapist, with his commitment, and love for the community, fostered healing within the groups of people he supported. As a member of his support group, I witnessed how all of the members' lives changed for the better. I believe as a result of the experiences we shared together, many have found or are on the way to living out their life purpose.

People can make a deep personal change if they desire. I have heard some say, "People cannot change" or that something is "just a person's nature." If you have a strong faith, success in your professional life, and decent personal relationships, yet you still do not feel you are living the life you want to live; consider connecting with a group of people that are committed to each other and is on the same path of seeking a deeper understanding of self. Participating in a support group allows you to communicate freely with like-minded people who can help you as you attempt to discover your true self. My decision to work on my marriage and then find a counselor who believed in the power of group work changed my life.

The approach of accountability and consciousness made a huge difference in my ability to see myself more objectively. As I think about the personal struggles I encountered in my life, I now know that it was how people perceived me that caused the conflicts. Knowing this has helped me to become the self I always wanted to be. Having a group of women who understand and support each other has been invaluable to my healing. We agree on how to give feedback and support to each other in ways that promotes growth. I look forward to our monthly meetings as we discuss what is going on in our lives.

Is There Something You Want to Accomplish?

As you begin your journey to self-awareness, consider the following: Do you have second thoughts about your experiences? Do you ever think, I wish I had not said that, or, I wish I would have said that? Maybe you have never thought about any of your interactions with others, but you are completely unhappy with your personal and professional relationships. No matter the struggle in your relational situations, think about another way of looking at your life. Consider that you are responsible for what is happening in your life. You can make your interactions with others fail or succeed by how you engage with the people around you. No matter how a person is treating you, being open to seeing your responsibility over what you are experiencing with others is powerful.

I am not promoting a specific way to understand yourself, but I am saying you can find your way in life when you least expect it. To start on this path, consider the people in your life whom you enjoy, respect or care for. Folks you feel the most comfortable with are a good starting point. When you have things you struggle within your relationships, empower others to give you their authentic feedback. Let them tell you how they see you and then trust the information.

Try going to people in your life and asking them to tell you what they think about you and your behavior in different situations. Give them the permission to give their general perspective of you. This can be eye-opening and freeing. The part of my life that I was not open-minded and it kept me stuck, and did not allow me to live up to my potential. It changed the trajectory of my life when I decided to accept my truth.

There is power in feeling control over your life, but when you are aware, alert, open and engaged it is much more affective for all the people you deal with day to day. In order to heal, you must change your behavior. Many people feel as if they have NO control over what is happening to them. Those that are rules-driven tend to be judgmental and lack the ability to process what and why they are having negative interactions with people. (Trust me, I know!) I know from my own experiences that the change has to come from within.

Once I woke up and gained a deeper understanding about myself, things changed in my relationships with others. Slowly people who made me feel valued came into my life. It was important for me to go back and heal some of the relationships with the people that I had bad experiences with, by being open and honest with them about my role in our conflicts. I must admit that some of those relationships did not survive. It pained me that I was unable to rebuild those relationships and I took responsibility for my part in those breakdowns. It was important for me not to repeat those negative behaviors with my new relationships and encounters with people. I told people that if I did something to offend them or made them feel uncomfortable, to let me know how they felt so that we could work through it.

Helping people to become more aware is what I do for a living now. I know I am not the only person yearning for more rewarding connections and transparency within relationships. I know that many women are suffering in silence and hiding behind their careers or their families, their social status, or their beauty. We all have deeply personal goals we would like to accomplish. The more you know about yourself, the more you will know what you want, what you think, and how you feel. By taking a deeper look into myself, I have reduced the stress in my life tremendously and am a much happier person. I no longer blame others for my reactions and I think about what I might be doing to contribute to difficult situations. There is power in not taking on other people's pain and/or sadness, which you can learn more about in my forthcoming books, *The Friendship Lab* and *Let's Talk About It!* Being self-aware will help you to build stronger relationships and will change your life for the better. It worked for me and I know it can work for you.

About the Author

Tia Buckham-White

Tia Buckham-White is the founder of Notre Internationale, LLC an Atlanta based firm focused on Self-Awareness, Personal Support Coaching with a focus on Group Support and Team Engagement. Notre helps people, teams and organizations become more Self–Aware. The goal is to promote business effectiveness and strengthen productivity. As a personal support coach, group facilitator, and public speaker, Tia works with individual groups, small groups and midsize organizations.

Along with public speaking, Notre offers one-on-one support, monthly support groups, and quarterly workshops. The monthly group meeting support following: Single Women, Single Women whom never been married with no children, Married Women, Mature Women in 10+ year relationships, Couples, and Entrepreneurs. There is a focus on managing difficult relationships whether personal or professional and understanding how your perspective of yourself affects your bottom line.

Tia has 15 years of corporate experience in Information Technology and Sales and Customer Support. Her open minded approach and understanding of corporate culture has served her well in dealing with technology teams and business users.

Visit www.notreinternationale.com for more information

The Authentic Woman: Stilettos, Suits and Sweats™
10 Secrets to Living a Happy, Successful, and Balanced Life

T. Renee' Smith

The savvy female entrepreneur wants it all—a successful business, a solid marriage, well-rounded kids, a healthy body, a clean house, a fabulous wardrobe, and to-die-for stilettos. She is empowered, bold, driven, and—above all—a superwoman. She takes the bull by the horns to accomplish her goals, but often loses herself and the passion which inspired her to be an entrepreneur, solopreneur, and mompreneur. As a result, she experiences burnout, often has limited cash flow, and is overwhelmed with managing the day-to-day business operations.

Can you see yourself in this description? Are you losing sleep, missing family events, spreading yourself too thin, or worrying about increasing revenues? Do you have a vision of accomplishing great things in your business, but for some reason lack the traction to get it done? If you answered yes to any of these questions, you are not alone. As a busy entrepreneur, wife, mom of two active young boys and an adult daughter, I know exactly how you feel.

If you are ready to turn up the volume in your life and have more fun while growing a profitable business, this chapter is for you. Discover 10 secrets that include love, laughter, and humility in your personal plan for success. Together, let's bring your vision to life. It's time to put you on your path to:

WIN BIG IN BUSINESS AND LIFE!

MY STORY

When you imagine the ideal female entrepreneur, I'm probably not the type of person that comes to mind. Low self-esteem, major insecurities, paralyzing fear—"These are not the qualities of a self-assured businesswoman!" you say to yourself, and you're right. But if you look back many years ago, that was the person staring at me in the mirror. At 19, this hesitant, unconfident version of me thought she had met her knight in shining armor. After building several successful businesses with said knight and enjoying a life of luxury—including million-dollar homes, expensive cars, exotic vacations, and designer clothes—I was convinced I had reached perfection.

Unexpectedly, the phone rang at 2:00 am, and I was dethroned as queen: the fairytale was over. I found out that my knight was married and that his new wife (of 4 months) was pregnant and expecting their first child. My life spiraled out of control. I supported, loved, and placed this man first in my life for more than a decade. I even alienated my family, endured mental and verbal abuse, and placed my life on hold so that he could pursue his dreams.

This may sound bad, but it got worse. Fast forward a few

months and I found myself on the wrong side of the law. I lost everything.

******

The beginning of my 30s did not start off well. I spent my 30th birthday in a movie theater by myself, watching Tyler Perry's *"The Diary of Mad Black Woman."* I cried and had a good ol' pity party. But I'm here to tell you that the end years of my 30s were rocking. I spent my 39th birthday spoiling myself at the spa and having dinner with my amazing husband and kids.

It is possible for you to go through hardships—abuse, infidelity, bankruptcy, molestation, divorce, failed business, abortions, imprisonment, failure—and still start anew. Yes—although I say start anew, versus start over. You have gained wisdom from every situation you have experienced, and each is a lesson you can use to start a new life today.

I've come up with 10 secrets that will help you on your journey of living an authentic, happy, and abundant life. Are you ready to begin?

Okay. Let's get started.

10 secrets to living a happy, successful and balanced life

Secret #1 - Be clear about what you want in life

In order to Win Big in Business and Life, you must be clear about what you want. Most people never reach their full potential during their lifetime because they don't have a set destination in mind—a definitive goal that they can work towards. If you don't know where you are going, how will you know when you have arrived? You must be very intentional about creating the life you want, and this starts with creating a specific objective.

I remember when I started to dream and create my vision board. I was sitting at home with very little money, single and working for someone else. Now—if you had looked at my vision board, you would have seen dozens of pictures displaying published authors, famous motivational speakers, and business gurus. I was dreaming *big*. I was envisioning myself as an international speaker, a highly sought-after life and business coach, and a New York Times best-selling author. My vision board represented my dream house, my dream car, my dream husband, and my dream kids. Was this my current reality? Absolutely not! But I knew that if I ever wanted to see these dream materialize in real life, I had to first envision it in my mind and feel it in my heart.

Think about what you really want in life. If failure was not an option for you anymore, what would you attempt to do? This is the mindset you need to have when you are creating a vision for your life. At a vision's beginning, many people get stuck thinking about how they are going to bring it to reality (instead of simply enjoying the possibility of it), and this often results in a fear-induced paralysis and an inability to move forward. Don't start by trying to figure out a strategy of how to make it happen. For now, engage in your fantasies; you'll have time to work on them at a later date.

If you have placed your vision on the back-burner, re-ignite it. It's time for you to rekindle your aspirations and dream big! While it is great to dream, our visions cannot become reality until we put some action behind them. That is why, for me, DREAM means:

Dedication. Responsibility. Education. Attitude. Motivation.

Secret #2 – Shift your mindset

It is finally time to live like the rock star that you are. Are you ready to stop putting everybody else first and finally take some time out for you? Then let's work on that mindset! The life that you are currently living is a direct reflection of what you think about yourself and what you tell yourself on a daily basis. If you are living an abundant and happy life, that is because you consider yourself to be living that kind of life. If you believe you are living a mediocre life, you are, because your mind is currently wired to believe that statement (despite your circumstances).

To change a negative outlook, gaze into the mirror and tell yourself how wonderful and smart you are. Tell yourself that you are valuable and a work in progress, and do this on a daily basis. Of course, if you have been telling yourself something different for the last 20 years, it is going to take your mind some time to adjust to this new train of thought. Remember: Positivity breeds positivity. Negativity breeds negativity.

In order to shift your mind, you have to change your environment. If you are spending all day absorbing negative input, that is what will stay in your mind. Right now, you are doing what you know. Therefore, in order to see different results in your life, you must learn to adopt a different perspective. Alter your mind by changing the things you read, see, and say on a daily basis. And get yourself a coach, a mentor, or a friend to serve as your accountability partner. He or she will ensure that you make the necessary changes in your life to alter your mindset.

Secret #3 - Set priorities and boundaries

You must set priorities if you wish to live a balanced life. For me, my priorities are my relationship with God, my self-care, my husband, my children, my family, and then my career. Am I always successful at keeping my priorities straight? No, but at least I have a reference point to go back to, which helps keep me balanced. I can't say yes to everything in my business because then I will be saying no to my family. It is not realistic to say yes to everything in family and business, either, because that means saying no to myself. It's a tricky little dance that you have to constantly work on. But the more you work on it, the better you will become.

Pull out a piece of paper and draw a line down the middle. On the left-hand side, write down (in order) what your current priorities are. On the right-hand side, write down what you want your priorities to be. Are they the same? If not, you may have to make some real decisions about what you need to do in your life to rearrange your priorities. Remember, consistent action brings results.

Secret #4 - Design your business around your life

Many of us miss the boat right here—including myself. For years, I designed my life around my business, fitting family and friends in where I could. I would always place my business before my relationship with God, myself, my spouse, or my children. I would work to exhaustion and have nothing left to give to my family. Often, my husband would tell me that he felt like he got the leftovers of my attention. I would pour so much into my business that I didn't have anything left for my family.

Eventually, I had to learn to design my business around my life, not the other way around. And you, too, will have to decide what kind of life you want to live. Do you want to work 3 days a week or 5 days a week, 20 hours a week or 40 hours a week? Do you want to work from home, in an office, or at Starbucks? Be clear about the life that you want to live, and mold your business to fit your lifestyle.

Be authentic about the type of life that you desire. As a mother of two busy boys, I need to have flexibility to ensure that I have plenty of time for homework, trips to the park, and story time. I also need time to make sure that my husband (a military man) has a clean castle to which he can come home to. In my case, I made the decision that I needed at least a half a day per week to run errands and handle all of the domestic issues related to my household. In designing your ideal life, choose what works best for you and your family.

Secret #5 - Open up your spirit

Look to a higher power or source for guidance. Open yourself to God's (or the universe's) plan and timing in your life. Realize your direction may come in a different package than you expect.

Before I got married, I had a 12-page, single-space typed list of all the attributes that I wanted in a husband. And God asked me if I was all of those things that I wanted in a mate. If not, how could I expect them from someone else? I changed my prayer and said, "God, prepare me for my husband and send me who you want me to have." Don't you know my husband came to me in an unexpected way (and in a different package)? If I wasn't open, I would have missed the greatest husband and father to my children.

Open yourself up to God's (or the universe's) plan and His (its) timing. Live a life of gratitude. Every day, wake up and be thankful for your breath, your vision, your hearing, your movement. Set aside time for daily affirmations and meditation. Two of my favorite affirmations are: *I have all the time, energy, and resources that I need to accomplish my goals, and, I am a wealth magnet; people love to give me money and do it often.*

Secret #6 - Be an original version of yourself

Don't live your life being a carbon-copy of someone else; be an original version of you! You don't need someone else's approval of you. Instead of seeking outward approval, find inner confirmation. Approve of yourself and validate yourself; that's all you need.

I remember when Oprah said, "The minute I stopped trying to be like Barbara Walters, I found my own authentic voice." If you try to be like someone else, you will just be an imitation of them. I have seen so many coaches take the materials of someone else and just reuse it. And they wonder why they aren't having success! It is because they are not speaking from their authentic voice. Yes, you will gain things from your mentors, friends, and coaches—but don't try to be them. Be you.

Secret #7 – Choose healthy relationships

The foundation of all your relationships is shaped by your relationship with God and yourself. Knowing that you are valuable and worthy is essential to all your relationships, because it prevents you from being mistreated by others. I once heard Paula White say, "I want to be celebrated and not tolerated in any relationship that I am in." I love that. You have to know your own worth and value, and when you do, own it. Everything else will follow suit.

Remember that we teach people how to treat us. If you are not good to yourself, why should anybody else be?

Whenever I reflect upon the relationship I had with my ex-boyfriend of 10 years, it saddens me. That was a time in my life when I didn't understand my own worth and value as a woman. I allowed him to disrespect me in so many different ways. He was controlling, verbally and mentally abusive, manipulative, and selfish. I was raised sheltered and was quite naive. I would give and give until I was operating on my reserves. As a result, my self-esteem was at an all-time low. It wasn't until many years later (after that relationship ended), that I really realized part of the reason why he treated me that way, was because I allowed it.

Understand that you are special and need to take care of yourself so your emotional tank remains full. I often tell people that when you are in a service based business, you pour into people all day long. If you never replenish yourself, your emotional tank will remain empty. And you can only operate on reserves for so long.

Surround yourself with people that motivate, encourage,

and celebrate you. You want people that will be honest with you about your flaws and areas of improvement. Additionally, you want to make sure that they build you up as well. The ceiling on your business is the ceiling on your intimate and personal relationships. Support from your significant other, friends, and family directly affects your success in business.

Secret #8 - Act in spite of fear

I have heard several explanations of fear Face Everything And Rise, Forget Everything And Run, and False Evidence Appearing Real. I personally love Face Everything and Rise. Stop making excuses because you are afraid. Act while afraid; act when in fear. In order to succeed, your desire for success has to be greater than your fear of failure.

One thing I do for my clients (and myself) is every time they give me a reason why they *can't* do something, I ask them to turn it right around into a can. For example, one client told me, "I can't grow my business because I'm already working 70+ hours a week and not spending enough time with my family." I told her to turn it around and give me all of the reasons why she can grow her business: "I can grow my business by delegating some of the work that I do, so I can have more time to focus on my family and build my brand."

Fear is a natural part of life. But don't let it paralyze you. Take action, and do it while afraid.

Secret #9 – Fail forward

Let me just say that I love John Maxwell, a leadership expert and speaker; he totally changed the way that I think about failure. Maxwell's advice is for us to fail forward. He states that "the difference between average people and achieving people is their perception of, and response to, failure."

Most people are never prepared to deal with failure, but failure is going to knock on your doorstep regardless of how much money you have or who you are. Instead of being afraid to step out and do something because you fear failure, embrace it. Failure is just a second opportunity to make a better impression.

When you encounter life's difficulties, turn them into stepping stones and keep pushing forward. Get out of your comfort zone and take calculated risks. If it makes you feel any better, I have had more failures in business than I have had successes. Has this stopped me from trying? No. I fail forward. I learn every lesson that I can, whether it is from a failed business or a failed relationship. Failure makes me stronger and wiser. Every day, I continue to fail forward.

Secret #10 – Forgive often

Forgiveness is an open gateway to healing. It is giving up the hope that your past could have been any different than it was. Forgiveness must first start with ourselves. Get rid of your negative self-talk: *By 30 I should have been married with 2 children. By 40 I should have had a millionaire dollar business. I never should have stayed in that relationship that long.* You cannot change your past. It has happened, and it is time to move on. Forgive yourself for all the mistakes and bad decisions that you have made. It is a part of life's lesson. Learn from it and grow.

You Can Do This

A lot of people ask me how I overcame an abusive relationship, legal problems, bankruptcy, failed businesses, and many other set-backs in life. What was the secret to remaining so positive? First, realize I am no different from you or any other woman. I've struggled with low self-esteem, dysfunctional relationships, negative self-talk, self-doubt, and mediocrity. There were many times in my life when I didn't think life would get better. I thought this was the life that God had for me.

However, I made a choice to have a better life. Yes, it is absolutely a choice. Sometimes I took two steps forward and three steps back. But I kept moving. Sometimes I was successful and sometimes not so successful. I used things that people would consider failure and just learned there was a different way to do it next time.

The good news is you can create the life that you want. Living an authentic and fulfilling life is within your reach.

I would love to help you on your journey, so feel free to contact me today at www.treneesmith.com to schedule a complimentary discovery session. Remember, you can **Win Big in Business and Life.** It is absolutely possible. Let's start today and do it together. Be blessed.

Visit www.winbiginbusinessandlife.com for more information

Forgiveness of others is letting go of the need for revenge and releasing negative thoughts of bitterness and resentment. Offenses are a part of life, but relationships can be healed and restored through forgiveness. Forgiveness doesn't mean that you forget the offence that happened—especially if it violated you; forgiveness means you are releasing yourself from being held hostage by your past. Forgiveness is a process: the more you do it, the easier it becomes.

About the Author

T. Renee' Smith

T. Renee' Smith is a certified coach, founder and Chief Empowerment Officer at iSuccess Consulting, Inc.™: a coaching firm that helps entrepreneurs remove the obstacles that prevent their companies from unlimited scalability. Many entrepreneurs invest years into building a business, but never figure out how to step away from it when it starts to consume all their time. They fear burn out, have limited cash flow, and are overwhelmed with managing day-to-day operations. Through T. Renee's proven systems, The AUTHENTIC Success System,™ The GROWTH Success System,™ and The RESULTS Success System™. She teaches business owners how to grow a purpose-based business that brings in consistent income and provides freedom to live an authentic, happy, successful, and balanced life. As a result, her clients are able to free up their personal schedules and have more time to focus on family and personal interests while their company still continues to grow and develop profitably.

Today, drawing from her experience with Fortune 500 companies, nonprofits (including Children's Healthcare of Atlanta), and many small firms, she builds businesses and personal champions with a focus on living an authentic, abundant, and peaceful life full of purpose and passion.

T. Renee' has been featured in many national and local publications including Cosmopolitan, Entrepreneur, and Atlanta Tribune magazine. She believes anyone with a vision, determination, and persistence can WIN BIG IN BUSINESS AND LIFE!

Investing In Your Brand Value

Kim N. Carswell

You don't get paid for the hour. You get paid for the value you
bring to the hour." – Jim Rohn

If you are the person who people come to for advice, whether
it's the perfect dinner recipe or the easiest way to get around
town, then you have a brand. Everyone has a collection of
traits that attracts others for a myriad of reasons; however
most do not take control of their personal brand or work
it to their best interests. Branding is a great way to harness
your talents and expertise in today's digital age of Google
and social media. It is also a way for others to invest in you,
because first and foremost people do business with other
people.

The importance of having a thirst for knowledge of self is
essential to advancing your positioning in the workplace and
for growing your business. Far too often women overlook
or are unaware of how a yearly professional development
strategy (action plan) can impact whether goals are achieved.
Now, let's jump right into a few components of Pink Power:
A MasterMind Conference Women (PPMC) PinkPrint for
Success. PPMC is a large scale event dedicated to bringing

the necessary resources needed to empower and advance women in business and in the workplace.

Meeting the Right People

In the book *Tipping Point* by Malcolm Gladwell highlights the role of the Connector.

> *Connectors are very influential people who know a lot of other people – they have extraordinary social connections. But Connectors are important for more than the number of people they know, they are important because they know people in so many different groups and niches. They can bring your message to so many worlds you don't belong to.*

Felicia Phillips of Fillips International Inc. and I were bitten by an awesome connector, Tess Vismale. She knew it was long overdue for Felicia and me to meet. Our mutual friend is a celebrated event professional, who became weary after having similar conversations with two people who were in the same profession. Felicia and I had yet to meet, but we were both focused on women initiatives and taking our businesses to the next level.

Tess threatened Felicia and I to meet one another. It felt like a heavy dose of ostracism being placed upon us. Ironically, a few months before the threats started flying, Felicia and I became Facebook and LinkedIn friends, but that was not enough. All bets were off once Tess realized we lived on the same side of town and graduated from the same university. Bottom line, we needed a face-to-face encounter like yesterday!

Prior to the ultimatum, I was in a groove …or so I thought. I had a seamless phone intro system in place while I worked on my second book, accelerated my training sessions, and cared for my personal branding client list. But for some reason I never inquired about Felicia's number--a clear causality from too much Social Media complacency. Since my valuable friendship was put on the line, I immediately had to devise a "Get out of the dog house" scheme and shot Felicia a quick Facebook message which read:

Kim N Carswell

Hey Lady, We need to get together via phone or in person. You know the same leprechaun who has pushed me to reach out and make it happen.

Here is my mobile 404.xxx-xxxx. Forgive me for the typos (corrected to save face)

Felicia Phillips

Yes!! Lol…I just finished getting scolded. I'll call you when I leave the studio.

Kim N Carswell
Okay cool

The rest is history. Thanks to Cheddar's restaurant, their awesome fish tacos, and our mutual desire to elevate women into a place of purpose, we drafted the cornerstone of PinkPrint for Success. With Felicia's grand scale expo and sponsorship expertise, and my commercial and personal branding proficiency, Pink Power: A MasterMind Conference For Women (PPMC) was born. Special note: the "F" in "For" is capitalized because it symbolizes "For Women By Women", but rather than creating a knock off FUBU brand (For Us By Us) by launching a FWBW movement, I just kept it highlighted throughout the branding process. Hint this is the first of many branding antidotes that will be outlined in this chapter.

Expand Your Reach

Soon after our initial meeting it became evident that our networks were ripe to increase exponentially. We met with the WNBA's (Women's National Basketball Association) Atlanta Dream, IKEA, Microsoft, and two local entities within (ABWA) American Business Women's Association to begin building the framework for the event. As with anything the frame began to change as more business leaders became aware of the goals we were attempting to reach.

One of our main objectives was to help women on and off the court. Partnering with the Atlanta Dream not only provided an awesome platform (first LEED Certified sports Arena) it allowed us to support a broader range of women who are striving for the best in their industry. Ironically, basketball is one of my favorite past times and I briefly played on the varsity team in high school. I grew up watching Clyde "The Glide" Drexler, Bernard King, Dominique Wilkins and Julius "Dr. J" Erving perform magic on the courts. Etched in my mind are Dr. J's endless hang-time and foul line dunk shots. Interestingly enough, I also have a son who is a basketball enthusiast. From the young age of 2 years old, he showed signs of superior eye-hand coordination and a ecstatic reaction to seeing a basketball court. Once I shared Pink Power's collaborative story involving the Atlanta Dream, he lit up with facts and stats about the female players in the WNBA. He also offered astute male comparisons to both active and hall of fame NBA players. To my surprise, his enthusiasm and wealth of knowledge exposed the depth and scope of how I took the sport for granted when it came to being engaged with women basketball athletes.

Rapidly, it also became evident, this new partnership would serve as another opportunity to improve and learn more about the commonalities among women transitioning between careers and professional athletes. Hence, the Pink Power MasterMind event became ripe for the Professional

Athlete Panel at Philips Arena in Atlanta. Overall we wanted relevant and actionable content disseminated by women who are at the top of their game. To allow women to see the common thread of obstacles, struggles and triumphs from a diverse group of women within a wide range of industries.

Behind the MasterMind Format

I absolutely love movies, they give me business inspiration in ways to showcase people's passion leading them into their purpose. One of my film favorites that came to mind when thinking about PPMC was the movie *Chocolat'*. The film starred actress Juliette Binoche as Vianne, a vivacious traveling entrepreneur, who along with her young daughter sets up a Chocolate Shoppe in an old-fashioned and starchily religious French town.

When the two ideologies of fasting during the Catholic Lenten season and the craving to indulge in sweets clash, Vianne doles out her exotic passion for suggesting the perfect ingredients to the most decadent chocolate treats for each villager. She deployed her knack for listening to hometown women and knowing how to bring out the best in them. Ultimately, she changes the lives of the villagers, her male antagonist's as well as her own.

Subsequently, I thought it would be great to create a MasterMind Conference centered on doses of digestible content (Yes, I'm a foodie too) for both career and business women. We took into consideration that people's time frame to hear information has shortened drastically and with the success of TED's 15-20 minute talks, I decided to give local speakers the opportunity to expand their brand by delivering salient information that audiences can use during and after the event. Designing multiple networking opportunities throughout the conference was also central. It is far more effective when people have time to engage one another soon after the content is delivered.

Brand Check One, Two…

Panelists were another important element to showcasing the array of experts in topics such as Science, Technology, Engineering, and Math, or STEM, Power of Green, Branding, Media and the professional athlete's discussion. Since I work with countless numbers of clients who are in transition whether self-imposed or not, the biggest challenges is to discern what their true purpose is versus what they have been paid to do by past and current employers.

My definition for transition includes those who are looking for promotions within their current company. Knowing your brand value leads to a win-win outcome for both the employer and employee. Each is getting more and the working professional has a better pulse on the types of ways they add value to the company and ultimately their lives. This is why it was imperative to not only have PPMC address the needs of a small business owner but to also close the gap between the career professional and entrepreneur.

In these lean times it is important for women to understand that companies appreciate employees who have an entrepreneurial spirit. One of my speaking topics includes a talk called "Handle Your Business", which highlights ways employees can treat their talents and abilities as profitable commodities leading into every employment decision. It outlines how important it is to take stock of your value during the hiring process and encourages job seekers to enter into a well-negotiated contract agreement to improve the financial outcomes for the company and their private lives.

When is a good time to check on what your brand is worth? It is best to keep a pulse on how you're adding value to the world. Some may not think that they're impacting the globe by just doing what comes naturally. However I often share with my clients that they were given certain talents for a reason and often share my shortcomings as an example of how I honor their gifts, just as they honor mine; which is knowing how to pull out *Patterns of Purpose*. Yes patterns of purpose lead you to why you were put on this earth and how best to use your talents.

We often hear people mention their passion for art, music, serving the poor or disenfranchised. All are great gifts that people share; however I take it a step further by noting that our passions should lead to our purpose. Your passion brings you joy, whereas your purpose brings countless gifts to others. Basically why we were put on this earth. Why did we go through certain pains and obstacles? What did we learn from our triumphs and challenges? How can you transfer your life's lessons to benefit a business or entrepreneurial venture?

Fundamentally… Who Are You?

As a working professional it is imperative to chart the trajectory of your career. In my branding book, *Resume Branding Strategies for Getting Noticed in 10 Seconds or Less: SECOND EDITION,* I outlined the difference between personal branding and the importance of branding your career:

Personal branding involves the essence of who you are and how to market your personality, credentials, and experience to the world. It's your reputation and what people say about you when you leave the room. It's what people say about you when they have to describe you to peers, colleagues or people in their professional networks.

At first glance, many people frowned upon this notion because it felt inhumane, distant, and trivial. Once career experts began embracing the concept of marketing one's skills set, advising job seekers to evaluate who they are and what they want, and exploring ways to reach one's employment goals, people started to warm up to the idea.

With personal branding you have the opportunity to steer the course of how others judge your character after meeting you for the first time--whether it happens to be in person, on paper, or online. People who know their personal brands are getting hired and or promoted more often and faster, despite the state of the economy.

Take the time to invest in reframing how the world sees

your talents and expertise. Whether it's updating your resume, professional bio, LinkedIn profile, or all of the above. Defining an engaging personal brand is essential. Know your value and make time to assess it as often as possible. Mingling with experts is always a great way to check where you fall in a certain industry or discipline. Once you've carved out your niche it will be easier to navigate in networking environments such as day-to-day interactions, workplace situations, and professional development conferences.

At the Pink Power MasterMind Conference For Women, speaker Pennae shared with attendees how she was two people; one was the professional multi-million dollar face of fame and fortune, the other was a person with bouts of of homelessness, and physical, emotional and drug abuse. Her talk was riveting to say the least. It depicted her resiliency and ever maturing relationship with God throughout it all. Overall her story was compelling and made the audience take stock into how they were channeling their past into the future.

As you explore ways to define your brand, first time must be taken to discover the real you. Eckert Tolle has a wonderful book titled, *The New Earth*, which highlights the differences between who we truly are and our EGO. The latter is why most self-described, experts, gurus, and mavens reached out to command the PPMC stage and were denied. We sought ladies who had superb storytelling ability when sharing their successful corporate or entrepreneurial journeys.

Only a Few Are Ready

One of the main areas of concern for women in the

workplace was the lack of female representation on Fortune 500 advisory boards. The pattern has spread beyond the traditional corporations. Even companies within the Social–Techo fields such as Facebook, Google, and Twitter board seats are dominated by men. Instagram is a little more secretive and only list's one person on their board of directors. To no surprise it is a male, Matthew Cohler. PPMC was designed to speak to this disparity and the event format was going to represent the power of lifting up women who blazed a path for other talented women to follow.

As the official "Speaker Seeker" for PPMC it was a revealing to encounter the number of women and few men who wanted to grace the stage. It was a challenge to select the best people to represent PPMC's brand this year and hopefully the subsequent years to follow, both domestically and abroad.

For the MasterMind portion it was imperative that only women delivered the content. We had a few men sponsor workshops on Day one, but the decision was made to keep their headshots off the website. Although men were in the minority, the brand imaging had to remain consistent. Why? Far too often large conferences had too few women thought leaders and favored men in seeking expertise on topics that many women occupy. I felt this was an insult to injury because it's better to lift up women trailblazers than give another man a platform to reinforce what women are lacking. In many cases they're missing male advocates who can champion their perspective and mentors who cultivate talent versus gender in the workplace.

Gender became a double-edged sword. Since the event was for women and about women, many assumed that since they fit the physical requirements it qualified them to speak. It was such a painfully wrong assumption. When vetting talent one of the first interactions was digital via email or social media. The herds of ill-defined brands were disheartening to say the least. Here this was a group of people who classified themselves as professional speakers. My prime target was women experts to pour into other women who were ready to absorb great content and change their circumstances as it related to leadership, mentorship, and or entrepreneurship. The digital image was the deal breaker. As we all know "A picture says a thousand words." Without strategic branding, we don't know what words come to mind when viewing a photo and or website. In many cases the interested speakers were not ready and should have considered attending the Branding Panel moderated by The Atlanta Journal-Constitution's (AJC) Managing Editor, Monica Robinson.

Investing in a quality photo is essential. Let me define what a professional photo consists of excellent lighting, an engaging pose, and 300 dpi (Dots Per Inch) quality for commercial printing. It does not just stop there… Be sure to have a picture that displays your personality. This is not an easy feat for photographers to capture unless you tell them.

For the record, I do not enjoy taking pictures at all. But it is a necessary evil if you're a professional speaker, business owner, and the like. So I had to research good ole' Google to retrieve captivating images of others and hired a celebrity photo artist, AC, to take my pictures. He knew in advance about my issues. I thought it was only fair to alert him of my adverse reactions to self-photography. It has nothing to do with how I view myself, it had more to do with preferring to be behind the scenes. Operations is my area of expertise and seeing how people and processes work hand-in-hand in various situations is my thing. So when it was time for me to decide who to align my brand with its important to gauge their expertise with my shortcomings. AC made me feel so comfortable that one of my favorite shots was a candid picture of me doubled over in laughter. Bottom line…Not liking to do something is never an excuse for not doing.

Spend time looking for the right person to take your photos, especially if you're an aspiring speaker. Event producers want to see you on a stage engaging their audience by sharing great content. Make it easier for them to showcase your expertise in their marketing materials and PR campaigns.

Do not forget to strategically place your commercial grade pictures on every professional bio and online by using them as profile photos on Facebook and LinkedIn.

The Right Marketing Makes a Difference

As stated earlier everyone has a brand. The question is whether or not you're taking control of it. One of the ways to do this is to invest in branding your persona. I have watched countless professionals fail to take advantage of networking windows and miss opportunities because they don't know their true market value or where to sell it.

What I have found is that people have major challenges with marketing their brand identity. This appears across the board with employees, writers, speakers and entrepreneurs. It is a misnomer that your work will speak for itself. No you have to craft the words yourself or hire a professional to do it for you. Either way you have to take control of the personal brand messaging process. Define the brand alignment rationale, spell out your brand's attributes and benefits to working with or for you.

Word of Mouth Marketing (WOM) is fundamental to building your brand. Most people are familiar with the reach of social media networking, but fail to design a strategy to support it. In essence, it is a platform and tool to spread the word about you, your products and or services. It's what I like to call your digital voice. A key element to keep in mind is that your message must be consistent with what's out there in the digital space.

In one instance a couple of friends referred another woman to speak at PPMC. One of them shared her contact information and I followed up by performing a brand assessment by looking at her website and social media presence. The referred speaker had a lovely and personable picture, but her reach appeared very limited. A few of the components I factored in when deciding who would grace the stage was: 1) Are people interested in her topic? 2) Was it compelling?, and 3) Could the experts draw a crowd? My initial analysis was to send a "Decline Email" to the speaker because I concluded that the answer to all three elements was No. Needless to say my friends were stunned.

They knew I was looking for speakers and could not fathom why their recommendation was turned down. After a few feverish conversations, I spoke to the prospective speaker and explained my conclusions. Guess what… The person I spoke to on the phone was not the person who received the brand assessment. But how could that be? Easy, my friend sent only one of her many email addresses and telephone numbers. Not only was the speaker in the middle of a brand renewal and career transition, she used three derivatives of her name throughout the digital space. Ironically one of them I was connected to via Facebook. What does this mean?

Keep your network up to date on your brand positioning. Perform periodic checks "Circle Backs", where you go back through your network to see what's happening on their end, educate them on your present initiatives and discard old content. WOM is excellent way to get your name out there, but for those who do not stay on top of their brand, it can be disastrous. It can essentially prevent you from achieving your goals.

Investing in your brand as outlined in the PinkPrint for Success, begins and ends with you. Revisit the advice laid out in this chapter as often as possible. Chart ways to strengthen how your network views and represents you. If you have yet to build a network, start today. Make the decision to become the "Connector" who can partner dynamic people together who will ultimately change the lives of many. ***Be better than the brands you admire...***

Visit www.personaaffairs.com for more information.

About the Author

Kim N. Carswell

"Your past does not define you---it refines you." ~KNC

Decades of business operations experience in corporate America and higher education led Kim N. Carswell to start Persona Affairs in 2001 when she serves as Chief Engagement Officer. In addition Kim is the Co-Founder of Pink Power International Center For Women, Inc. and counsels clients worldwide. Kim is an engaging conversationalist who has a passion for exotic teas from around the globe.

At the heart of it Kim is a brand catalyst who loves to use her training and conflict management expertise to guide executives, rising professionals and entrepreneurs, who have lost their luster, back to their true market value. She authored two career guidebooks: *Resume Branding: Strategies For Getting Noticed in 10 Seconds or Less*, that help readers define a digital and corporate brand. The leading social media platforms (Facebook, Twitter, Pinterest) selected Kim to participate in numerous business beta testing projects and was she awarded the "Top 1%" Linkedin Users distinction in 2013. In addition, Atlanta Area Council of the American Business Women's Association awarded Carswell the coveted 2014 Women of the Year.

Kim draws from her business acumen and counsel that has been used by various commercial and educational institutions with personal branding, conflict management and social media needs, such as: American Society of Civil Engineers, Atlanta Convention & Visitors Bureau, Delta Airlines, and The King Center for Nonviolent Social Change. Kim currently sits on the Advisory Board, and is a Guest Lecturer for Georgia Institute of Technology's School of Interactive Computing along with a number of the Top 50 corporations from Fortune's 500 list.

For further information, or to book or talk with Kim N. Carswell, contact: **engage@kimncarswell.com**

Persona Affairs, LLC
3900 Crown Road, #161870
Atlanta, GA 30321
1.888.331.4447
www.personaaffairs.com

Conclusion

We hope reading this book was an invigorating journey of insight, purpose and fulfillment. Each of us has shared a piece of ourselves that will leave you with a new perspective on how to win in business and in life. Pink MasterMind is best used as a tool to assist in designing and committing to your very own PinkPrint success. Remember that everything you have experienced has led up to this very moment.

Hopefully after reading this book, you have a clear understanding of our MasterMind approach to charting a better course of action for obtaining the life you desire. Once you begin looking for people in your personal and professional network to collaborate with, doors to new opportunities will open more frequently. Often times when people take a moment to reflect, they discover that what is needed to prosper is within arm's reach.

Shift gears and enhance your communication style on and offline. Social media and texting dominate the world we live in, but there is no substitute for face-to face interactions. Take time to evaluate your inner circle of friends and colleagues. Circle back and identify resources that you may have overlooked in the past, because now you are looking through a different lens.

Don't forget about the importance of personal branding.

As you work on defining a brand it will be easier to authentically tap into your boldness and beauty. You have unique talents and personality traits that make you stand out from the rest. Self-awareness is key to unlocking how you contribute to the world around you. Begin operating through positive consistency patterns at work or in your business that will expand your brand identity to attract more people.

Shift your mindset and reflect on what you desire in life. Define what success will look like, set some growth goals and get an accountability partner, a whole-hearted person who will not let you skirt your way out of fulfilling your purpose. Life happens, but when you have people encouraging you to be the best, it makes a big difference.

Remember, failure is not who you are, but it is a result of a series of actions. Fortunately a number of the choices you make are the jewels that lead you straight to your success. It is just a matter of reframing your thoughts and forgiving internal and external mistakes. Do not get stuck in the past. A great philosopher named Agathon once said, "Even God cannot change the past." Transition your thoughts to the present. Order your daily steps by building a path that quickly discards self-limiting beliefs along the way of claiming an authentic life and achieving a successful future.

Most importantly, think about how you can contribute to those around you on a higher level. Become a mentor or sponsor to women who can benefit from your insight and influence. There is something to be said about sowing seeds in fertile ground, pouring into someone who is ripe for guidance and mature enough to take action based on your advice, resources or expertise. Sometimes we just need someone to believe in us and provide powerful encouragement. The key to PinkPrint Success is in you. So, respond quickly to what you have learned and put it into action.

About The Publisher

Asta Publications was founded in 2004 and takes pride in providing excellent publishing services to first-time authors, entrepreneurs, veteran writers, corporations, and organizations.

Asta Publications believes that everyone has a story to tell and will work with you to turn your idea and/or manuscript into a professional designed book.

Visit Asta Publications online at www.astapublications.com for more information. Call (800) 482-7190 to speak with one of our publishing experts who can help you to achieve your publishing goals.

You can also find us on the following social media platforms:

Facebook
www.facebook.com/astapublications
Linkedin
www.linkedin.com/company/asta-publications
Twitter
www.twitter.com/astapubl/

CPSIA information can be obtained
at www.ICGtesting.com
Printed in the USA
FFOW01n2235040215
10849FF